Praise

Areva Martin brings to light the many lies that women are told to talk us out of our power and possibilities. In this powerful book, she motivates us to reimagine who we can be by stepping outside of limitation and bringing others with us. The issue of gender equity is addressed boldly in this text by someone who has lived out her words with inspiring fortitude. This book is sure to activate the leader in women from all walks of life.

Dr. Thema Bryant | Professor of Psychology, Pepperdine University, Psychologist and Author

A well-written, engaging, and often brutally honest book about women in the workplace and society at large. Many books in this genre have become outdated after the COVID-19 pandemic, racial reckoning, and the #MeToo movement... so thank goodness for *Awakening!*

Astra Austin | Co-Executive Producer/Writer, "Dr. Phil"/ CBS Media Ventures

Areva has always been a FORCE in the empowerment of women! In this book, she gives women simple tools to live their fullest lives and create satisfying careers. Whether you are an entrepreneur, a non-profit leader, or a woman looking to enter a new career, you've got to pick up this book!

Shaun Robinson | Emmy Award-winning journalist

Tearing down the system and rebuilding a new society feels like a dramatic solution...until you read *Awakening*. Areva Martin makes the point for why we need to think bigger and fight for equity, not equality. I learned so much while reading this book - and you will too!

Tamara Nall | CEO & Founder,
The Leading Niche

Areva's observations and keen insight are spot on! As a working mother in a competitive field, I found the issues facing the remarkable women featured in *Awakening* to be all too familiar. Rather than dwell on the negative, Areva offers us tools to address these slights, injustices and micro aggressions in ways that are positive, productive and life-affirming.

Shawn Holley | Partner,
Kinsella Weitzman Iser Kump LLC

Awakening is a careful exploration of inequity and inequality. So many of us can identify with so many of these stories. Areva Martin details a list of specific problems and provides real-world, user-friendly solutions. This is a smart and accessible book that gives readers a positive path forward.

Jessica A. Levinson | Professor,
Loyola Law School & Host, "Passing Judgment" Podcast

Areva has marshalled a wealth of data to demonstrate how far women have come and how far we still have to go to achieve equity in America. She shows how gender bias hurts all of us. By placing women at the center of her analysis, Areva has devised a number of fresh approaches to begin tackling gender inequity and creating a more just society for all. This book is a must-read.

Dr. Niambi M. Carter |
Associate Professor, Howard
University, Washington, D.C.

Areva has done it again! Written another must read for all of us women seeking truth and inspiration. Whether you're just beginning your professional journey or looking for a long overdue reset, *Awakening* is the book you need to have on your bookshelf.

**Judy Belk | Writer, President/CEO,
The California Wellness Foundation.**

The discussion about women and gender equity in the workplace has been a sensitive subject among men for a long time. Areva Martin provides concrete and fascinating information on how men can benefit from gender equity and show healthy support for women in their lives and workplaces.

**Christian F. Nunes | National President, National
Organization for Women**

Book clubs, listen up! This needs to be on your list next year. The talking points on gender equity and women in the workplace will bring everyone over to your next meeting with questions, stories, and maybe some arguments! *Awakening* will get everyone talking.

**Paul Gunn | CEO,
KUOG Corporation**

When I read this book, I can't help but think of my mom, sisters, and female friends. I am excited to bring this book to them and have conversations that we have (unfortunately) never had before! *Awakening* really opened my eyes.

**Kristin Cripps | Developer,
Entrepreneur, Award Winning
Author and International Speaker**

Put this in a time capsule and people in 2051 will have a fascinating look into the struggles women faced in the workplace, the Black Lives Matter movement, and other social issues that defined 2021. What an informative and interesting read!

**Rick Orford | Co-Founder &
Executive Producer at Travel Addicts Life, and
bestselling author of The Financially Independent
Millennial**

This book, by the esteemed, brilliant, incredible Areva Martin, speaks directly to the heart of what I (and so many women, especially women of color) endure in the "professional arena". Reading Awakening, I just feel so seen. The more I read, the more I feel it, and the more I know I am never alone. Please do yourself a favor; pick up this book, follow the exercises, and do the work to heal yourself. Your mental health depends on it, and I thank you Areva Martin for articulating your truth, our shared truth as women, and for giving us tools to heal.

**Dr. Alfiee Breland-Noble | CEO
and Founder, The AAKOMA Project**

Leave it to Areva to, yet again, address and advocate for a critical issue such as gender equity. She's a force for fairness. Awakening should be required reading for all young girls, boys, women and men - an inspiration for this generation and those to come. The more information women are armed with the better our chances for professional success.

**Ianthe Jones | Executive
Producer/Showrunner, Facebook
Watch & Steve Harvey**

Navigating the corporate workplace and career landscape has never been easy for women and mothers. I am one of the millions of mothers who walked away from the corporate world and chose entrepreneurship because I was frustrated and unable to find that fantastical "balance" as a working mom. I wish I had Areva's book back then for the guidance, straight talk, and hard facts she compiles and presents in a painstakingly honest yet accessible way. Thank you Areva for saying all the things that need to be said and for speaking to everyone.

Kimberly Seals Allers | Award-winning journalist, Author, The Mocha, Manual Series & The Big Letdown: How Medicine, Big Business and Feminism Undermine Breastfeeding, Founder, Irth App

Tear down the system! This book is like watching Wonder Woman or Black Panther. You just want to recognize the superheroes in your life and build a new world. You're a superhero, Areva!

Robbie Montgomery (Miss Robbie) | Celebrity Chef, Owner of Nationally Acclaimed Soul Food Restaurants, Sweetie Pies & Author of Sweetie Pie's Cookbook Soulful Southern Recipes from My Family to You

This is a must-read corrective and expansion on Sheryl Sandberg's Lean in. Areva Martin invites us to lean further into the underlying biases, stereotypes, and racist assumptions that prevent women from succeeding. With both personal and well-known stories of women who have faced these obstacles, Martin illustrates not just what the problems are, but offers practical solutions for dismantling these unjust systems so that all people can have equal access to success. Awakening is for all women – and men – ready to envision and create a flourishing society for everyone.

The Rev. Dr. Leah D. Schade | Assistant Professor of Preaching and Worship, Lexington Theological Seminary

In my work in hospitality, I know so many people who can relate to this book. Areva includes self identifying women, from all walks of life: women who have come from lower socioeconomic backgrounds, women of color, LGBTQIA women, and women with disabilities are all considered. Mothers and women who choose not to have children are considered. Most importantly, men aren't excluded from the conversation but they are called in to support the women around them. Thank you, Areva, for speaking to everyone.

Lynnette Marrero | Co-Founder, Speed Rack, Bar Director LLama Inn, BKLYN | LLama San NYC

Areva is like your best girlfriend who isn't afraid to say what's on her mind. And what's on her mind? Gender inequity! This is such a necessary book for men and women to learn something new and reignite a fire that has been under many women in the corporate space.

Cheryl McKissack Daniel | President & CEO, McKissack & McKissack

It's been more of a whirlwind than I ever suspected in relaunching a Blackbird work + wellness space — love to show you when it's closer to complete. I have been wanting to sit down and write an in-depth BC style review, but in an effort to support more expeditiously, I adopted one of your already great review templates.

Brigid Coulter | Founder and CEO Blackbird House

AWAKENING

Ladies, Leadership, and The Lies We've Been Told

Areva Martin

Leaders Press

Leaders
Press

ISBN 978-1-63735-013-3 (pbk)
ISBN 978-1-63735-012-6 (ebook)

SIMON &
SCHUSTER

Print Book Distributed by Simon & Schuster
1230 Avenue of the Americas
New York, NY 10020

Library of Congress Control Number: 2020925502

Dedication

To my two daughters and son that they may live in a truer world.

Contents

Introduction xvii

Section 1. The Lies..1

1. The System Will Recognize Your Hard Work 3

2. Your Value Is Not Determined By Your Beauty......13

3. You Can't Be A Working Woman And
   Raise A Family 23

4. Women Are Inferior...35

5. The System *Works* —It Just Needs To
   Be Tweaked 45

Section 2. Exploring The Problem 57

6. How Did We Get Here? 59

7. Mentors, Men, And Leaning Into
   Closed Doors...75

8. Expectations, Norms, And Culture
   Are Holding Us Back..91

9. Rebuilding The System Benefits
   Everyone 103

10. Working Within The System Is Not
    Enough... 117

Section 3. Solving The Problem 125

11. Reimagine And Reflect 127

12. Address The Lies 143

13. Use Your Voice! 151

14. Bring Men To Your Table 161

15. Congratulate Women Who Are
    Winning.. 171

Contents

Conclusion **179**

Acknowledgements **183**

About the Author **187**

https://arevamartin.com/books/

https://arevamartin.com/books/

Introduction

Kamala. Tulsi. Marianne. Elizabeth. Amy. Kirsten. In 2019, these six women stepped up to the plate and announced their run for president of the United States. The spotlight was on them as they stood on a national stage in debates that had seen very few women before them. Watching them gave me hope for myself, for my daughters, and to future generations of women around the world.

But lingering around those feelings of hope was a full range of emotions, including sadness, fear, and frustration. The presence of these six women on a national stage was a reminder that it *is* unusual to see women on a major party's ticket. The United States of America witnessed the vitriol and sexism that Hillary Clinton faced in 2016. What would a woman, especially a woman of color, be subjected to if she were to run against Donald Trump?

I saw, in the eyes of the women running for president, the everyday women I had encountered throughout my career. Law and nonprofit work put you face-to-face with women who are fighting for justice. They are fighting for themselves, their sisters, their colleagues, and women all around the world. Women fight every day against sexual harassment or sexual abuse, unjust pay disparities, and other barriers that have prevented them from exercising and enjoying the unalienable rights promised to all people.

The first few months of the 2020 election were historic, but outside of the debate stage, women seemed to be moving backward. When COVID-19 hit, many women felt forced to leave their jobs to care for their children. Unemployment rates for women hit 15.5 percent. In the final months of 2020, women struggled to get back to their jobs, but still faced serious challenges of balancing childcare responsibilities and regaining the forward momentum they had had in their careers pre-pandemic. Unemployment rates for Black and

Latina women significantly trailed that of white women. The story of women choosing childcare over a career, out of choice or out of societal pressure, is not new. Every woman I know has told this story in one form or another. These stories have greatly impacted me and shifted my focus when it comes to the fight for gender equity. That is why I decided to write this book.

Defining the Problem

I cannot sit around waiting for changes to be made in the workplace. In 2021 and beyond, we must awaken and rise together. But in order to do that, we must take an honest look at the society we are living in.

This book is separated into three different parts: defining, exploring, and solving the problem. In the first part of this book, I highlight five key lies that we have been told. Our society is built within a system that was designed specifically to hold women back. This system has spread many lies about women, work, and our role in society. By exposing these lies, we can begin to create a more equitable society for all people.

Exploring the Problem

The second part of this book takes a look at where we are today, what women have done to fight back against the system, and what we face moving forward. Despite worldwide movements to combat harassment and fight for representation, women still face a lot of barriers on the path toward equity. Everyone must be a part of the fight to dismantle and rebuild the system - but as we explore the possibilities of achieving this goal, we must understand that not everyone understands what it means to live in a more equitable society.

Solving the Problem

The third part of this book focuses on the solutions that we can use to build the society we want to give to our daughters, granddaughters, and future generations. Although you will find actionable items at the end of every chapter, this section will dive deeper into strategies, tactics, and suggestions for solving the problem. Not all of these solutions will fit into your lifestyle, industry, and career goals. That is okay. Take what you need from this book, and leave the rest to the others fighting for gender equity. This book is the story of all women who are fighting for success; don't compare your chapter to someone else's. Although this book contains stories from colleagues, friends, and fellow CEOs, know that your path is uniquely your own.

Rebuilding the Society We Want to See

Throughout this book, I will examine the stereotypes, mindsets, and expectations that hold women back from achieving gender equity. I choose to say "equity" rather than "equality." As I explore the system and share solutions to this problem, I am aware that I must retroactively account for the barriers that women have faced financially, socially, and even physically.

Here's an example of why I strive for "equity" instead of "equality." You ask two people to lift one hundred pounds. The first person has been training to lift one hundred pounds their entire life. They have no problem accessing a gym with weights and a personal trainer who will guide them and keep them safe. When they tell other people that they want to lift one hundred pounds, they are congratulated and given protein shakes to keep them fit.

The second person simply hasn't had those opportunities. They were never allowed in a gym and they couldn't buy weights. Personal trainers refused to take them on as a client. No one would assume that this person would one day be asked to lift one hundred pounds.

Inaccessibility prevents people from realizing their true potential. "Equality" is giving both people the opportunity to lift one hundred pounds. Both people in the example *could* work toward lifting one hundred pounds, although the first person is more ready *today* to lift one hundred pounds than the second person. Access to resources and support from others played a huge role in their present abilities. Equity accounts for the shortcomings that a person may have faced in the past. Equitable solutions "even out the playing field."

Our society has lied to us, either telling us that women do not deserve equity or that our current standing in society is equal to that of men. Women have undergone centuries of discrimination, trauma, and setbacks due to these lies. We need to catch up and rebuild a society where these setbacks do not occur. This book will address the ways that we can fight back, and why our mindset should zoom out and look at long-term goals that dismantle and rebuild our entire system. It is not enough that we have six women on a debate stage, running for the highest office in the United States. We must rebuild society so that when we see women in the C-suite, or getting elected to office, or earning more than men, they are no longer milestones or history-making moments.

I hope to inspire you to move forward in a way that allows you to live out your ambitions, reach all of your career goals, and collaborate with other women destined to make a large-scale change in the world.

Before We Begin

This is a book that can be picked up, put down, studied, and discussed. You probably won't read it just once! But before we dive into the actions and strategies that will change the world, we must set the scene. Confronting the lies told by the system can be exhausting. Take your time; this process is necessary to move forward and make the appropriate changes. Getting through Section One brings the rewards sprinkled throughout Sections Two and Three. This is the reality of advocacy and activism: hard work, emotional labor, and even pain must precede success or revolution.

The world has been living a lie, failing to see the true influence and presence of systemic sexism in every aspect of our society. We have believed the lies the system has told us for far too long. If you picked up this book, you heard the rumblings of change urging you to expose the lies and live out your truth as a powerful, successful woman. I heard them, too. Now is the time for us all to awaken and rise.

SECTION 1.

The Lies

CHAPTER 1

The System Will Recognize Your Hard Work

My godmother and grandmother taught me that I would always have to work twice as hard as everyone else. They exposed this central lie to me early in life. We are told that all we have to do to get ahead in life is to work hard.

Why did my godmother and grandmother tell me that I had to work twice as hard? One, I was a girl. Two, I was a Black girl. In order for me to get ahead, I would have to be twice as good and work twice as hard as my counterparts. If I didn't show up for work early, stay late in the evenings, and work weekends, I would be left behind. So, I showed up for work early. I stayed in the office way past sundown. All of my weekends were dedicated to work, and I never turned down an assignment because I was too busy. Private time? Personal time? What was that? I had to give 110 percent just to see the success that I wanted for myself. According to my godmother and grandmother, working hard was the key to reaching that success.

But here's something my godmother and grandmother didn't tell me. They didn't tell me about the old boys' network. They didn't tell me about how hard racism, nepotism, favoritism, and sexism pushed back on the idea of my success. They didn't tell me that the stale prejudices that built the foundations of our country were such strong barriers. No matter how hard I worked, I would never be seen as equal to my white male counterparts. These men were never told that they had to work *twice* as hard. No extra hours were required to make them twice as revered as the Black girl next to them. My white male counterparts were rewarded simply because they showed up. They were paid fairly because they were expected to be the breadwinners of their family. They were promoted because their grandfather owned the firm or their father played golf with the "right people."

All I have to do is work hard, and I'll be on the same level as the white men next to me, right? That is a lie! No matter how hard I worked throughout my career, barriers fundamentally built into our society have prevented me from truly being an equal. I'm not the only one, either. Women all over the country have run into these barriers. Pay inequity, harassment, the "choice" between motherhood and a promotion; all of these barriers mitigate the hard work we put into our careers. Meanwhile, our male counterparts are rewarded *just* because of their sex. The system doesn't just fail to recognize the hard work of women around the country. The system also rewards men, regardless of whether they work hard or not.

I do not want you to walk away with the wrong idea about me. I don't regret the values that were instilled in me from my mother, grandmother, and godmother. I'm very proud of my work ethic, and I passed that work ethic on to my own kids. But I do regret that girls, especially girls of color, are told this lie about hard work. We need to tell them that yes, hard work matters, but they have to recognize the system. The system doesn't always reward hard work because the system was built with sexism and racism at its core. Sometimes you can be twice as good and work twice as hard as the white man next to you. You're still not going to get that promotion. That man was going to get that promotion all along, no matter how hard you worked.

Instead of recognizing your hard work, the system will encourage you to work harder while paying you less. This system has long been in place, and the only way to start tearing it down is to expose it.

The System Will Make You Work Harder

I was awakened to this lie long before I started my own law firm or began writing this book. When I was applying for jobs coming out of law school, I knew I had worked hard. I was graduating with honors from Harvard University, and I was at the top of my class. Before Harvard, I had graduated with honors from The University of Chicago. What other credentials did I need? But I didn't get every job I applied for. I was turned down for multiple jobs, even with a Harvard degree and top credentials to back me up. If I had been a white male graduating top of the class, with honors from Harvard, I don't believe I would have had the same experience.

When I started working in law, this awakening became even more clear. I saw that the long hours I worked and the sacrifices I made weren't going to pay off. Hard work wasn't the key to success that I thought it was. I started attending conferences and meeting brilliant, successful women who had left their profession after being turned down for partnerships. They did everything I thought I had to do to be successful. These women also worked 12-, 14-, or 16-hour days. They gave up everything. When it came time to get that partnership, there was still something missing.

As I listened to more women talk about their experiences in the workforce, I realized I wasn't that special. There was nothing unique about my experience. The women who had been turned down for partnerships also went to Harvard, Yale, Columbia, Stanford, and The University of Chicago. They were overachievers, they worked hard, they did everything. But they weren't represented at the top. If you look at the hundreds of years that women have been in the legal profession, women have dominated. Law school graduates have been equal in terms of men and women for the past 50 years. But the number of women who have made partner, especially in cities like New York and San Francisco? Abysmal. Women have always worked hard, only to be denied opportunities, promotions, and higher pay. Why? Our sex.

I was twenty-eight or twenty-nine when I saw this lie for what it was. Yes, hard work is important, but there was something more to this picture. I realized that there were barriers holding women, especially women of color, back from getting the promotions they want and the pay they deserve. And I couldn't break this barrier down by being inside a system built to oppress me. I had a better chance of leaving the firm I worked for and working on the outside to break those barriers. So that's what I did.

At twenty-nine, I left that big corporate firm. I gave up that big, high-paying job. My family thought I was crazy, so I had to explain that it was a dead-end job. I had nowhere to go. If I wanted to see the success that I envisioned for myself, I would have to start my own law firm. I had few barriers of my own when I first started: I wasn't married, I had no kids, and I had little debt. If I totally fell on my ass, I had a Harvard degree and could find employment in another field. My work ethic allowed me to build a successful law firm and career, but this only happened when I stepped outside of the system and built that career for myself.

A Black woman with Harvard credentials is still a Black woman. A white male graduating with my credentials would have been able to enter many spaces that were simply closed off to me. Now, I have enjoyed (and continue to enjoy) the educational privilege that I had. My credentials have given me lots of opportunities, and I've had a wildly successful career. But all that aside, I have not been given the same opportunities as my white male counterparts. What's the difference? Our race and our sex. Therein lies the lie. The system will not recognize your hard work before it recognizes your race and your sex. In many cases, it won't recognize your hard work at all. I set up my own firm because no one was going to give me a partnership.

This is the story of my awakening, and the awakening of many women around the country who have endured similar treatment. Once we recognize the lie that we have been told, that the system will reward us on hard work alone, we can start to move forward and look for solutions to work within this lie or tear down the society that has fed us this lie from birth. The system will *not* reward us for hard work alone. Despite how hard any woman works, especially a woman of color, structural barriers and systematic biases will prevent us from achieving the level of success that we know we can reach. You can't avoid these barriers, no matter how hard you work or how good you are. No amount of Ivy League degrees, titles, or hours at the office can penetrate these systems of biases. They are the systems on which this very society is built, and they are set up to tear us down.

The System Will Pay You Less

Kristen Jacobson's Story

Kristen Jacobson knows far too well that hard work doesn't reap the rewards that the system promises. She is one of the many women who shared their experiences with me as I wrote this book. These experiences, ranging from small microaggressions to appalling acts of sexism, may feel all too familiar. They serve as reminders that all of us have been duped by a lie: that the system will recognize (and reward) our hard work.

Jacobson was working as the director of marketing for a cardiac medical device company. She was reassigned to co-lead the Food and Drug Administration (FDA) approval team with the clinical director. The team worked to get the company's first FDA approval, and after months of eating dinner at the office and working around the clock, the company got the approval. This was a make-or-break moment, thanks to the leadership of Jacobson and her co-lead. To thank her, the company gave her a "bonus..." of $1,000. One percent of her salary. In contrast, the CEO of the company thanked *himself* with a $100,000 bonus. Although Jacobson believed that the CEO deserved a bonus, in comparison, hers was an insult.

This, and other financial slights, became leverage when Jacobson negotiated for higher pay. Her boss, a woman, had decided to leave the company and left Jacobson with some crucial information. Both of Jacobson's male peers had been making double what Jacobson was making. Her team was responsible for all of the disposable sales and she had personally helped to close over 90 percent of capital sales even though they weren't directly in her purview. Yet, she was making half of what her peers were making.

Her boss promoted her to vice president (along with her male peers.) This gave her the opportunity to demand a discussion on salary discrepancy, as well as a raise. At the time, this was a big step for Jacobson. But looking back, she wishes she had discussed restitution for the years of underpayment. Jacobson's boss made the excellent decision to be transparent and proactive in the fight for pay equity, but the overall company culture drove Jacobson to eventually leave the field.

"It was not fair for me always to have to be in a position of requesting more compensation or having to justify or sell my worth and it wore me down. I left the company not long after discovering my salary was half the men's and didn't go back to corporate America as an employee. I chose to lead in other ways."

Kristen's hard work wasn't rewarded in the same way her male coworkers' hard work was rewarded. She had believed the lie that society told us about hard work. When pay discrepancies were revealed and she left her job, she was able to see the lie for what it was. The system never intended to recognize her hard work.

Mariah's Story

Of course, Kristin is not the only woman driven out of a company due to egregious pay inequity and a dismal reward for her hard work. A woman, whom I will call "Mariah," earned the role of an executive at a fast-growing, eight-figure company. Mariah was a rising star, earning three promotions in under two years. She was given a position where her input on hiring was certainly heard and considered.

Mariah had interviewed a man for a role at the company, and quickly saw a field of red flags. He was sexist, ageist, and appeared to be untrustworthy. On top of his apparent bigotry, the man asked for a salary that was triple Mariah's. If he were to be hired, he would also require that the company cover the costs of a cross-country move. She was adamant that he was wrong for the company and should not be hired.

You might know where this story is going. After Mariah had interviewed this man and given him a hard pass, she was sitting in a leadership meeting. She was told, to her complete surprise, that the man had been hired to work in the same position as Mariah. The company had accepted his demands. Despite Mariah's warnings, this man was also given a leadership role. It's no surprise that after he was hired, he was the subject of incident after incident. Mariah herself became a target of his harassment. When the company hired this man, they blatantly disregarded warnings of sexism and Mariah's input, ultimately to her detriment. She knew it was time to leave her position.

The story becomes *more* frustrating. When Mariah decided to leave, the company needed to find a replacement. Her team decided that her role would be replaced by two lower-level management positions and an outsourced firm. Once the hires were made, Mariah saw just how undervalued she had been at the company. One of the men in the lower-level management positions, a man with less experience, was offered Mariah's three-year earned VP salary. When Mariah had started at the company, she earned *half* of that salary, despite contesting it. Her gender was the only thing holding her back from earning two or three times her salary, a salary equivalent to men in the same positions. The system doesn't reward hard work fairly if you are a woman, *especially* a woman of color.

Mariah's story feels like a one-two punch. This blatantly sexist man was hired *and* he received triple the pay that Mariah was earning? No wonder women are fed up. This incident is one of many that speaks to how men and women perceive, identify, and (sometimes) prevent sexism in the workplace.

The System Is in Place, and It Needs to Be Exposed

Women have been told for years, for decades, that if we just work hard, we can get ahead. When women don't get ahead, due to pay inequity, demanding schedules, or biases within our own companies, blame is placed back on women. Why didn't we work harder? Why didn't we stay at the office longer? Why didn't we put our children in daycare, get another degree, or spend more time networking?

We have to stop asking ourselves these questions, as if our work ethic is the problem. I am a strong woman because I was raised by strong women. I am a hard-working woman because I was raised by hard-working women. I know you are, too. And yet, we have been led to believe that hard work is the one key to getting ahead. I worked my butt off, and although I did achieve some success, I faced plenty of barriers along the way. The barriers at my former corporate firm were impenetrable. I worked hard everywhere I went, but only when I saw the barriers of the system did I find my way around them and build my own business. I want you to see these barriers, too, whether they are at your corporate firm, in academia, in your organization, or even within your own home.

I am writing this book to expose the lies that we have been taught, starting with the idea that the system recognizes our hard work. The system will not recognize our hard work the way it will recognize a man's hard work. When we acknowledge this, we can work hard to fix it. You can't fix what you don't acknowledge. By recognizing this lie (and the many other lies that we have been taught,) we can expose the biased systems that are out there. We can see when they are working against us and make a plan to make the systems work *for us.* Kristen Jacobson and Mariah are both successful businesswomen. They worked hard, but they had to go through these experiences to acknowledge the lies they had been told and the systems that were working against them. Now is your time to do this, too. Now is your time to awaken and rise.

Awakening Action Item. Open your journal and spend ten minutes reflecting on your experiences with sexism in the workplace. What was it like asking for promotions? Do you feel like you have a shot at equal pay compared to your male colleagues? If you were subjected to harassment or unfair treatment, do you think your team would have your back? Reflect on these experiences and how they make you feel about your career, your coworkers, and your confidence.

CHAPTER 2

Your Value Is Not Determined By Your Beauty

"You're so pretty." How many times did you hear that as a girl? How early did you notice that pretty girls get more attention? The system doesn't recognize our hard work - it is far more likely to recognize our physical attractiveness. If women are beautiful, they are rewarded. They are considered to have a higher value. If women aren't beautiful, they aren't even acknowledged.

As we examine this lie, we find statistics that prove the pressure to be pretty is *real*. Studies show that women are rewarded, not for working hard or living by a moral code, but for looking good. Men don't face this type of pressure, and it benefits them in more ways than one.

Beauty *is* pain, that's no lie. But the tangible costs of going through this pain are rarely worth the value that we gain from adhering to society's norms and expectations for women. Those expectations, which benefit white, skinny, delicate-looking women, provide higher and more impenetrable barriers for women of color. When we consider these expectations, we also have to look past our makeup and hairstyles. Our value is determined by not only our beauty, but also our *delicacy.*

I have found myself spending hard-earned money and ridiculed for the color of my skin and the style of my hair. I'm sure that you have experienced taller barriers and trickier choices due to the way that you look and the way society expects you to look. All of these experiences are based on one big lie. In this system, your value is determined by your beauty, despite the body-positive ads that might try to tell you otherwise. Acknowledging the system requires that we acknowledge how much pressure has been put on women to be pretty.

The System Rewards Women for Physical Attractiveness

The system's connection between value and beauty influences the choices that women and men make in the workplace. In fact, this sexist lie influences us before we can legally apply for a job! Some would argue that sexism influences us before we are given a birth certificate. The idea of what it means to be a "man" and a "woman" is vastly different. If women aren't reaching the system's beauty standards, they're simply setting themselves up for failure. They don't just fail as a businesswoman or an entrepreneur, either. The system equates our physical attractiveness with our *womanhood*.

We have been told that a woman's value comes directly from whether or not she is physically attractive. If we're not attractive, we're simply not a good woman! In 2017, the Pew Research Center asked Americans what traits society values in both men and women. The results were not shocking, but showed a gap in how we view a "good man" versus a "good woman[1]."

- Thirty-three percent of participants said that society values honesty and morality most in men.
- Twenty-three percent said that professional and financial success were the most-valued traits.
- Ambition, leadership, strength, toughness, and a hard work ethic also made the top of the list.

[1] "Honesty Tops List of Traits That People Say Society Values Most in Men; Physical Attractiveness Top Trait for Women," Pew Research Center's Social & Demographic Trends Project, November 30, 2017, https://www.pewsocialtrends.org/2017/12/05/americans-see-different-expectations-for-men-and-women/pst_12-05-17-gender-02-00/.

- Thirty-five percent of participants said that *physical attractiveness* was the most-valued trait in women.
- Empathy, kindness, and the ability to nurture also made the top of the list.

Women constantly feel the pressure to not only be *physically* attractive. Tack on the pressures of running a home and caring for the kids and there is little room for career success, ambition, and leadership! These pressures can have a significant impact on the decisions we make at work and how we are perceived by both *men and women.*

Men are not free from expectations or pressures. But with a higher paycheck and fewer expectations to change their physical appearance, men can spend more time (and money) meeting the expectations placed on them. Honesty and morality, rather than physical attractiveness, are valued most in men. Honesty and morality are free. Physical attractiveness is (usually) not free. Women find themselves at a disadvantage immediately due to the societal pressures placed on us. In a country where the wealth gap has *doubled* in the last three decades, no one person can afford to be at a disadvantage[2].

The Economics of Beauty

Women don't need me to tell them that the pressure to be attractive can feel frustrating and overwhelming. Yet, when you see stats that say physically attractive people earn 20 percent more than "average" people, these pressures can also feel inescapable[3]. Women who look polished and adhere

[2] Juliana Menasce Horowitz, Ruth Igielnik, and Rakesh Kochhar, "Trends in U.S. Income and Wealth Inequality," Pew Research Center's Social & Demographic Trends Project, August 17, 2020, https://www.pewsocialtrends.org/2020/01/09/trends-in-income-and-wealth-inequality/.

[3] Jaclyn S. Wong and Andrew M. Penner, "Gender and the Returns to Attractiveness," Research in Social Stratification and Mobility (Elsevier, April 16, 2016), https://www.sciencedirect.com/science/article/pii/S0276562416300518.

to traditional beauty standards are simply doing what is expected of them. Women who forgo makeup, dress more casually, or wear their hair in an "untraditional" manner are subject to criticism. We are told that we look tired, ill, or simply unprofessional. Can't we focus on business, instead? Can't we get an equal paycheck, regardless of our cup size or how our hair looks?

No, we can't! Not in this system!

What do we do about these biases? Many women, whether they are conscious of these biases or not, respond to the lies told to them by breaking out the bronzer and keeping lipstick in their purse. But although adhering to beauty standards appears to be the "easy way out," it comes with a cost.

The Tangible Costs of Beauty

Physically attractive people earn a higher income than "average" people. But there is more to these stats than you might think. When the researchers involved in the study controlled for grooming, they saw that incomes were more even. Beauty standards are rarely achieved naturally. Women have to spend time, spend money, and expend a lot of effort to reach a level of attractiveness that comes with a higher income. If you don't have that time and money to spare, you're out of luck.

You have heard the phrase "beauty is pain." Beauty is also time-consuming and expensive. Surveys show that the average woman spends up to fifty-five minutes grooming herself before she heads to work. If she is also responsible for making her child's lunch, driving kids to school, or attending to household chores, she will have very little time left for leisure, rest, or passions! If time *is* money, we are spending a lot just to uphold traditional beauty standards. The playing field for men and women is far from level when you consider costs like these.

Even drugstore foundation or cheap mascara adds up over time. A 2017 survey from SkinStore revealed that women apply an average of sixteen cosmetic and skincare products to their face every day. This adds up to an average of $8 worth of products *every day* and over $200,000 of products in a lifetime[4]. Talk about a "pink tax!" We already know that women make less than men. But we don't always talk about how we *spend more time and money* on meeting the pressure to look attractive. Very rarely do we see the returns of this "investment." Physically attractive women are not outpacing men in terms of pay.

The System Rewards White Women for Their Beauty

We cannot talk about the pressure to be pretty, and what it takes to get there, without talking about Western standards of beauty. Beauty standards have typically been set by white people to affirm their power over minorities[5]. This requires minority women to spend even *more* money to adhere to styles of dress and hair set by people that don't consider their needs. Relaxers, straighteners, and other hair care products are not cheap, but many women of color feel the pressure to use them. For some women of color, these products are *required* to meet dress codes at school and at work!

Studies show that Black women are 1.5 times more likely to be sent home from work because their hair did not meet dress codes or beauty standards[6]. I know I'm not the only

---

[4] "How Much Is Your Face Worth? Woman's Daily Worth Value 2017 Survey - SkinStore," Skinstore US (The Hut.com Ltd., March 8, 2017), https://www.skinstore.com/blog/skincare/womens-face-worth-survey-2017/?affil=awin&utm_content=yieldkit&utm_term=Sub%2BNetworks&utm_source=AWin-143466&utm_medium=affiliate&utm_campaign=AffiliateWin&awc=15340_1598460786_33fc72d33fd643e3da6605562bb2725e.

[5] Leah Donnella, "Is Beauty In The Eyes Of The Colonizer?," NPR (NPR, February 6, 2019), https://www.npr.org/sections/codeswitch/2019/02/06/685506578/is-beauty-in-the-eyes-of-the-colonizer.

[6] "The CROWN Act: Working to Eradicate Race-Based Discrimination," The CROWN Research Study (Dove, April 6, 2021), https://www.dove.com/us/en/stories/campaigns/the-crown-act.html#!.

woman who has experienced this personally. Back in college, I spent a summer interning in the corporate department for a bank. I changed up my look by dying my hair red and was *immediately* reprimanded by a coworker. Not a manager, not a superior, but a coworker. He told me, "Oh, red hair now? That's not going to cut it in this environment."

Nothing about my hair was different. My hair was always neat and styled in a manner similar to other older, white women. The *only* difference was the color. But because I decided to make a simple change, I was reprimanded. Would a white woman be reprimanded in the same way if she was a redhead?

In my experience, no. No one else during my time at the bank was scolded for the choice to change their hair or deviate from the dress code. My choice did not impact my ability to be professional and excel at my job. Yet, I went home and changed my hair color again so I would feel respected in my position. I spent *more* time and *more* money to change my hair. This experience was frustrating, embarrassing, and not right, but it's part of the reality of living in a system where white women set the standard for what is (and is not) beautiful.

Fighting Back with the CROWN Act

When Black women embrace our natural hair, we are likely to be punished. Traditional Black hairstyles (cornrows, twists, and dreadlocks) have not only been banned in the U.S. Army, but also in schools throughout the country[7]. And the fight to end this ban rages on.

In January 2019, Senator Holly J. Mitchell introduced the Creating a Respectful and Open Workplace for Natural Hair (CROWN) Act to the California Senate. The CROWN Act aims to end race-based hair discrimination in the workplace or educational institutions. This would allow women of color to

---

[7] Areva Martin, "The Hatred of Black Hair Goes Beyond Ignorance," Black Hair Discrimination Can Harm Black Women and Men | Time (TIME USA, LLC, August 23, 2017), https://time.com/4909898/black-hair-discrimination-ignorance/.

wear braids, locs, twists, or Bantu knots as they receive an education or navigate the corporate jungle gym.

This act became California law in July 2019, but the fight is not over. In 2020, the CROWN Act was considered in twenty-five states, but never became the law[8]. If institutions continue to say that traditional Black hairstyles are unacceptable, how can they ever be deemed professional?

We spend considerable time and money at home just so that we can avoid being judged at work for meeting artificial standards that have nothing to do with our ability to work. How long are we going to keep allowing society to hold these unequal standards for men and women?

Your Beauty Is Determined by Your Delicacy

Beauty standards encompass more than just whether you wear makeup or not. Your tendency to smile, your weight, and your dress also influence how competent people perceive you to be. Maya Humes has seen her fair share of this pressure in politics. She told me, "In general, I think that physical appearance factors far too heavily into the way a woman is treated in politics. As someone who others love to talk about elected officials with, I hear criticism of Black women candidates that is based solely on their appearance all the time. People say things like 'Well, she looks angry every time she speaks,' or 'I think she's too pretty to be taken seriously,' or 'She's too overweight.' It's infuriating, and both men and women say these things."

Society's beauty standards for men and women reflect how society expects men and women to act and be. Our doe eyes, long hair, and skinny heels enforce the idea that women have always been regarded as the more delicate sex. Instead of driving hard bargains or arguing in the courtroom, women are expected to nurture and protect the children and home.

---

[8] "About," The Official CROWN Act, accessed June 7, 2021, https://www.thecrownact.com/about.

We look after people. Our interpersonal connections are regarded as more important than our efficiency at work. The emotions that come with nurturing and being empathetic toward others can have a serious impact on how we lead (and how we are perceived if we stray from our traditional role.)

When women defy these stereotypes, we are reprimanded. When we adhere to them, we are deemed unfit to lead. We saw this happen during Hillary Clinton's presidential campaign. When she first ran for president, people said that she was too stern and she didn't smile enough. If she cried, she was deemed too soft or emotional to handle the presidency. How can our society encourage women to show emotion, but then chastise them when they show emotion on a public stage?

You and I both know that the solution to meeting, much less escaping, these pressures is not simple. Showing up to work without makeup, setting emotional boundaries, and neglecting household chores may make a point but will not cause change on a large scale. Scowling, sneering, or doing anything less than smiling will only be met with criticism. To dismantle this lie, we need to let go of the expectations that are holding women (as well as men or non-binary people) back. We need to reimagine the value that we place on our beauty, what we consider beautiful, and how meeting those standards affects our ability to be seen as successful, confident women.

Awakening Action Item. Do not let pressure from society hold you back from reaching your full potential. Writing or reciting affirmations can empower you as you push back on the pressure to be pretty or to be perfect. Affirmations are short statements set in the present tense that affirm who you are:

- "I am a strong woman."
- "I fight for what I deserve."

- "I have the ability to change the world through kindness and love."

Write three affirmations, and put these words in a place where you can see them as you get ready in the morning or settle into your workday. Remind yourself, every day, of who you are and what you can do for this world.

CHAPTER 3

You Can't Be A Working Woman And Raise A Family

Why is our value determined by our beauty? Because the system was built for women to follow one path in life: find a man, have his children, and hold down his home. Today, not all women want to exclusively follow that path. The system, however, has not made many adjustments. The system continues to feed us this lie: that we can't be a working woman and raise a family at the same time.

This lie leads many women to put off having kids or to forgo them all together. Men can have it all, but women? No way. Between the tasks that we have at home and work, and the lack of compensation for working moms, women feel the pressure to choose their children *or* their career. The system makes us feel *guilty* about the thought of being a successful parent and a successful businesswoman at the same time. We're told that if we're working, we're bad moms.

The stories in this chapter come from both married and single mothers. It is important to note that the system neglects single mothers almost entirely, leaving them few choices to care for their family *and* navigate the corporate jungle gym. As we awaken and rise, we must remember to consider *all* women, whether they are single or married, caring for children *or* aging parents.

Men Can Have It All

The fear of leaving a well-paying job haunts many women who are determined to have a successful career. It is a fear that runs so deep it can prevent women from having a child in the first place. One of the top sacrifices that women make for their career is forgoing (or putting off) children. Between the ages of forty-one and fifty-five, one in three successful career women in the United States do not have children. In the corporate world, this number rises to 42 percent[9].

Of course, not all childless career women regret their choices. Some women simply don't want children. But rather than focus on the motives of women, let's zoom out. The decision to have children *or* a career is an "either/or" decision limited to women. Men do not have to make a "choice."

Men can have huge families, or they can remain a bachelor with no questions asked. They can have five kids, get divorced, and start all over again without sacrificing their career. When a man has pictures of children in his office, he is celebrated as a "family man." When a woman has pictures of children in her office, she suddenly becomes less reliable.

Women should not have to face a crossroads when they are trying to start a family or move forward in their career. Children or career should not be an "either/or" choice. As a mother of three and someone who knows the joys of parenthood, I feel the pain of friends who did forgo having children and now regret their decision. I feel the pain of my friends who, although they have achieved great success in their careers, realize that this fulfillment cannot replace or "make up for" the fulfillment of watching their child reach specific milestones.

Do I wish that my friends had been given more options to have children and achieve the success they wanted in their careers? Yes. Do I understand their choices? Yes. Women who choose to have children do face consequences for their choice. Statistics on the family pay gap and the

---

[9] Slyvia Ann Hewlitt, "Executive Women and the Myth of Having It All," Harvard Business Review (Harvard Business School Publishing, August 21, 2014), https://hbr.org/2002/04/executive-women-and-the-myth-of-having-it-all#:~:text=There%20is%20a%20secret%20out, States%20do%20not%20have%20children.&text=These%20 women%20have%20not%20chosen,in%20fact%2C%20yearn%20 for%20children.

work women do at home clearly show how women pay for their children in a way that men would never accept. These practices continue to uphold the lie that a woman couldn't possibly be a working mother *and* raise a family.

The Family Pay Gap

Imagine a world in which, after a heterosexual couple has a child, the father's pay decreases while a mother's pay increases. This seems impossible! Yet, statistics show that a family pay gap does exist. Once a heterosexual couple has a child, the gap in their pay increases significantly. Women experience a 7 percent wage reduction after they welcome a child into the world[10]. They may also be pressured to work part-time or leave their career and accept a new job with less favorable terms. Men, on the other hand, are likely to get a *bonus*.

Experts note that this gap is not equal for all families. Wage penalties for new mothers are much higher for women at the bottom of income distribution[11]. Wage bonuses for new fathers are much *higher* for men at the top[12].

[10] "Lack of Support for Motherhood Hurting Women's Career Prospects, despite Gains in Education and Employment, Says OECD," Lack of support for motherhood hurting women's career prospects, despite gains in education and employment, says OECD (Organisation for Economic Co-operation and Development, December 17, 2012), http://www.oecd.org/newsroom/lackofsupportformotherhoodhurtingwomenscareerprospectsdespitegainsineducationandemploymentsaysoecd.htm.

[11] Budig, Michelle J., and Melissa J. Hodges. "Differences in Disadvantage: Variation in the Motherhood Penalty across White Women's Earnings Distribution." American Sociological Review 75, no. 5 (October 2010): 705–28. https://doi.org/10.1177/0003122410381593.

[12] Michelle J. Budig, "The Fatherhood Bonus and The Motherhood Penalty: Parenthood and the Gender Gap in Pay – Third Way," The Fatherhood Bonus and The Motherhood Penalty: Parenthood and the Gender Gap in Pay – Third Way (Third Way, September 2, 2014), https://www.thirdway.org/report/the-fatherhood-bonus-and-the-motherhood-penalty-parenthood-and-the-gender-gap-in-pay.

Ironically, the reasons why new mothers see a wage penalty are the same reasons why fathers see a wage bonus. When someone who is dedicated to their career has a child, questions about their reliability, commitment to work, and stability come into play. The conclusions that employers make, however, vary for men and women. New fathers see a boost in pay because, as sociology professor Michelle J. Budig writes, "Fatherhood is a valued characteristic of employers, signaling perhaps greater work commitment, stability, and deservingness[13]." Motherhood, on the other hand, is interpreted as a sign that the mother is unreliable and ready to leave the workforce.

The Cost of Raising a Family

Why are women considered unreliable when they become a mother, but men considered *more* reliable when they become a father? The answer partially lies in old-fashioned sexism. The simple act of "becoming a parent" has become a reason to praise men and reduce women to their delegated role of an object whose function is birthing and caring for children.

Another answer is still rooted in sexism but has practical effects. Women simply spend *more hours* engaging in unpaid labor. This unpaid labor adds up physically, mentally, and emotionally. With only twenty-four hours in a day, how can we expect mothers to take on eight hours at work *plus* additional hours at home for which they are not being paid?

How much time does the average woman in the United States spend daily engaging in unpaid labor? Organisation for Economic and Co-operation Development (OECD) data says 271 minutes (just over four and half hours.) Men, on the other hand, spend 165 minutes engaging in unpaid labor (two and three-quarter hours.) These numbers are close to the average amount of unpaid labor that men and women partake in throughout all OECD countries[14].

---

[13] Ibid

[14] "Employment : Time Spent in Paid and Unpaid Work, by Sex," Employment : Time spent in paid and unpaid work, by sex

If you had an extra hour and forty-five minutes to prepare for work, be at work, or rest, what would you do with it?

Single Moms Aren't Considered

My experiences do not begin to cover the expectations and pressures put on women who are single, LGBTQ+, disabled, or other minorities. As we have opened doors for more people to join the workforce and gain full access to certain freedoms, we must shift our expectations when those people walk through.

Even when a woman is the breadwinner of her home (which is the reality for 49 percent of employed women), she faces pressure to take care of the home and children. If she works a full-time job outside of the home, she essentially works two full-time jobs once her additional household responsibilities are considered[15].

Splitting household chores with a partner is often easier said than done. You need a partner who is willing to see their role in raising children and cleaning the home. But for millions of moms throughout the country (a majority of whom are in the workforce), they simply can't split chores with a partner. They have no partner, just a child or children who need to be fed, bathed, and cared for. These single working moms still feel the pressure to look good, care for others, work full-time, *and* have time for rest, recreation, and hobbies.

What are the solutions for single mothers? Bring their child to work? This is not always possible. Spend $500 a month

---

(OECD), accessed June 7, 2021, https://stats.oecd.org/index.aspx?queryid=54757.

[15] Carrie Dann, "Poll: Workplace Equality Stalls for Women Even as Perceptions Improve," NBCNews.com (NBCUniversal News Group, March 22, 2018), https://www.nbcnews.com/politics/first-read/poll-workplace-equality-stalls-women-even-perceptions-improve-n859206.

on childcare[16]? Single mothers *may* be able to do this if they are in the right career, but note that this money might also be used to build wealth, pay off student loans, or contribute to a more professional wardrobe that women feel pressured to own. Could single mothers spend less time at work and more time caring for their child? Sure, but the setbacks that a woman could face for this "choice" are obvious. A woman's decision to care for her child, rather than spend time at work, is often interpreted by our society as an inability to commit to an employer. A woman's decision to spend *less* time with her child and spend more time at work is often interpreted by our society as an inability to parent. Single mothers, stuck with only twenty-four hours in a day, are truly in a "damned if you do, damned if you don't" whirlwind.

Is life automatically easier for working moms with a partner? Not necessarily. A study published in 2018 in *Demography* revealed that mothers with male spouses actually did *more* housework than single mothers (Pepin, Sayer, and Casper). There is no one, definite cause, although researchers believe that:

- Male partners *create* more housework for their female spouses (they are another mouth to feed and set of clothes to wash!).
- Single mothers are more tired and have less time available for housework.
- Children with single mothers are more willing or expected to pitch in.

The last point illustrates how important a team effort is to changing societal pressures on women. If children or partners are *expected* to take on household chores, a woman can spend more time concentrating on other things. If pay equity was achieved, a woman could afford to hire someone to take on

---

[16] "Historical Living Arrangements of Children," The United States Census Bureau (U.S. Department of Commerce, November 23, 2020), https://www.census.gov/data/tables/time-series/demo/families/children.html.

household chores. Maybe there is another solution that we have not yet considered. The system is working hard to make sure that we do not find a way around the lie it is trying to feed us. But as we search for large-scale solutions, we have to take into account the experiences that force us to create our schedules and make the "choice" between working and caregiving.

You Can't Be a Working Woman and Care for Aging Parents: My Story

As a working mother, I have had my fair share of encounters with this lie. My mother was sick during the period of time when I was getting my son's autism diagnosis and running my own law firm. I was living in California and my mother was in Boston. I was judged for not *literally* picking up my family and business and transporting them to Boston!

I spent a lot of time trying to convince my mother to move to California or back to our hometown of St. Louis. Many of her relatives were living in St. Louis, but they believed that *I* should be more directly involved with her care. Don't get the wrong idea. I was involved: I talked to her every day, I talked to her doctors regularly, and I went to visit her. But this was never enough. I felt immense pressure from family members, from my mother's friends in Boston, and from my mother herself.

Most of that pressure came from snide remarks. I felt like someone was always going out of their way to ask me when I was moving to Boston. People asked me if I knew how difficult a time my mother was having, as if I didn't speak to her regularly and care for her health. People made me feel like I had abandoned her or that I wasn't living up to their expectations.

My solution was for my mother to move to Los Angeles, where I had more support systems and could run my business while still taking care of her. She didn't feel the same way, although she did come to visit for three weeks. At the end of her stay, she wanted to move back home. I ended up convincing my housekeeper to move to Boston with my mother as her caregiver. That way, I knew my mother was under great care, and we could all live in the cities where we wanted to live.

This was the best solution, but I still couldn't shake the guilt that I was feeling. I was frustrated because my mother wouldn't move in with me. I was angry that her friends and family members expected me to abandon my business and move my family across the country. But above all, I felt guilt. Although my mother's friends and relatives felt satisfied with my solution of sending a caregiver to live with my mother, I couldn't shake these feelings. People acted as though I had made a choice that they approved of, but I didn't need their approval! My mother and I are both independent people who wanted to make our own choices. But when the system tells women that they have the freedom to make these choices, they are just telling us another lie. The system is built to make the choice for us, to motivate us to ultimately step away from career success to be a caregiver at home.

I share this experience because I know a lot of women in this "sandwich generation" who are under a similar type of pressure. They are caring for young kids, caring for elderly or sick parents, and they're being pulled in many different directions. The system has built the expectation that the woman, the mother or the daughter, is expected to drop everything to be a caregiver. No one expects a man to quit his job to care for an aging parent. No one expects a man to make the choice between family and work.

Kristen Jacobson's Story

Multiple women have shared moments in their lives when they were awakened to the lie that women can't work and raise a family. Kristen Jacobson, for example, was twenty-seven years old when she graduated from Stanford University Graduate School of Business (GSB). As she stood above the courtyard before graduation, a dean at the school asked her to defend the "worth" of continuing to maintain women in the Stanford Master of Business Administration (MBA) program at their current levels. Hearing the dean explicitly insinuate that women may not "belong" in the Stanford MBA program was shocking, but the dean insisted that there were "practical" reasons behind his arguments. He argued that, historically, the rates of women leaving the workforce were higher than men. With fewer women in the workforce, he speculated that fewer female Stanford alums would donate to the school or offer opportunities to future alumni. Was it "worth" investing in women's futures?

Jacobson fought back, arguing that the dean's speculations were baseless and the idea of reducing the acceptance rate of women was discriminatory. She believed she would be an example of the "ideal" Stanford alumnus who attended reunions, donated to the school, and excelled in her career. As Jacobson reflects back on her time at Stanford, this debate sticks out in her mind:

> What I did not bring up, that I now wish I had, was to challenge him and the other Stanford deans about what they were doing to research about why this phenomenon was happening and to address the systemic inequalities in the workplace that perpetuated that outcome. I am surprised that the crux of my argument was that it wasn't going to apply to me. I suspect it was because I was still an idealist who had not experienced or realized the impact of a corporate system not conducive to attracting, and as important, retaining and promoting women.

Women who feel "forced" to leave their careers to take care of children are the product, not the cause, of the system. The "choice" between motherhood and a career is the product, not the cause, of the system. These choices are put in place because the system is not built for women to have success in their careers.

Camille Proctor's Story

Camille Proctor did not initially intend to step away from corporate America after having her son. She was a single mother and had recently pivoted from a marketing career to working as a compliance officer for an Information Technology (IT) company. But as her son began to grow and display some developmental delays, balancing her job and motherhood quickly became tough. Proctor had to fight hard for an autism diagnosis; Black children are diagnosed with autism, on average, two and a half years later than white children[17]. Once he was diagnosed, Proctor faced even more setbacks. She now had to find support, childcare, and a community that understood the struggles of having a child who is both Black and on the autism spectrum.

Reflecting on this time in her life, Proctor told me:

> I sought out support and couldn't find any. I was always blown off by my questions about how to explain what autism is. How do I prevent my son from being harmed if he doesn't know how to communicate? No one understood or identified with what people of color go through, period! I was so tired and didn't have any support. My health suffered due to my anxiety. I felt helpless. Why wasn't there support for me and others like me? Why? I was a hot mess, but knew I would have to be that someone to forge change. Eventually, I walked away from a six-figure job because no one wanted to care for a child that screamed for hours upon hours due to separation anxiety, sensory issues, and other issues.

Of course, walking away from a six-figure job cannot completely alleviate a mother's anxiety, especially as the mother of a child with an autism spectrum disorder. The costs

---

[17] "Camille Proctor, Founder and Executive Director, The Color of Autism," BLAC Detroit Magazine (Ford Motor Company Fund, April 8, 2020), https://www.blac.media/people-places/camille-proctor-founder-and-executive-director-the-color-of-autism.

of raising a child with developmental delays are $1 million higher than raising a child without them[18]. We spend money on specialists, treatments, and even home renovations that accommodate our child's needs and preferences.

Camille Proctor could not rely on a partner to take her son to specialists or provide consistent at-home care. But even women with partners and women with neurotypical children find themselves making the same decision as her: to walk away from their job entirely. Fortunately, this story has a positive ending. Proctor identified the issues of systemic racism and sexism that prevented her child from getting the help that her family needed. Her experiences led her to start The Color of Autism Foundation, a nonprofit organization that helps to educate and support Black families with autistic children. Her awakening showed her a way through this tough period of her life. Our society wants us to believe that we can't be a working woman and raise a family. But that is just a lie.

Awakening Action Item. Are you ready to achieve what you want to achieve in 2021 and beyond? Set these expectations for yourself and the people who can help you get there. Schedule a conversation with your manager, partner, or childcare provider about your expectations for balancing work, parenthood, family time, or other areas of your life in a post-pandemic world. Be open, honest, and firm about any boundaries you want to set or tasks that you want to delegate to others.

---

[18] Catherine Pearson, "Study Reveals The Astounding Cost Of Raising A Child With An Autism Spectrum Disorder," Lifetime Costs of Autism Can Exceed $2 Million, Study Says (Buzzfeed, Inc., December 7, 2017), https://www.huffpost.com/entry/autism-costs_n_5474061.

CHAPTER 4

Women Are Inferior

The lies I have shared so far are smaller lies. They stem from the biggest lie of all: that women are inferior to men. Despite the evidence, throughout human history, that women are just as capable as men, the system continues to support this lie.

The system is not reality, but it has not been challenged on a large scale. There has never been threats of toppling or tearing down the system, even though it does not have to exist. We do not have to live by a system that tells this lie. By acknowledging and confronting this lie head-on, we see opportunities for change. The system has told the story of our society for hundreds of years and now it's time that we hit the world with a plot twist. We need a system that supports gender equity.

This lie has told women that they are not good enough to have a career and raise a family. It tells us that our value is defined by our beauty, not our brains or strengths. Even when we work hard and exceed the expectations placed on us, this lie ensures that we are not recognized for our hard work. Women are simply not worthy of a reward, this lie tells us. Why? Because women are simply inferior to men.

As we explore the consequences of this lie, remember: never underestimate your ability to change the world. The world has been built to work against you, but you are taking the first steps in changing that world and building a better system for yourself, your daughters, and all women.

We Aren't Expected to Reach the C-suite

This lie set expectations for me as a young Black girl growing up in a housing project. I was not expected to have a successful career as a lawyer.

At fifteen, I received some memorable career advice from my godmother. Now, my godmother loves me dearly. She knew how hard I worked and how far I wanted to go in life. But she also grew up in a world that believed the lie that women are inferior. She grew up in a world where women were expected to peak in "less respected" administrative roles, and "less respected" administrative roles were less respected because they were typically held by women. My godmother advised me to learn how to type so I could be a typist.

Of course, this advice was not memorable because it was critical to my career as a lawyer, advocate, and author (although I have become an excellent typist.) This advice is so memorable because it shows the conflict that many women have felt when setting career goals. As I reflect on her words, I feel conflicted. My godmother had positive intentions. She wanted me to work hard. The ability to type well was an employable skill that would allow me to become financially independent. Work as a typist or secretary would not be hard to find.

On the other hand, this message was limiting. Here I was, a fifteen-year-old girl who had intelligence, drive, and discipline. I was capable of graduating with honors from one of the most prestigious universities in the country. After that, I would go on to graduate from the most prestigious law school *in the world*. Yet, as a fifteen-year-old girl, I was told not to shoot for the C-suite but for one of the lower rungs of the company. I was not being groomed for leadership; I was simply encouraged to remain in administrative roles. My two older brothers did not receive this same advice. They were directed toward another path, one where they could pursue higher education, reach the highest levels of a company, and receive a higher paycheck. At a young age, girls are directed to one path and boys to a different path.

To this day, women, especially women who grew up in a housing project like me, may not be steered toward leadership roles or climbing the ladder at work. This misdirection may not happen consciously. The story about my godmother may feel like a story from an earlier era, but women still face a similar set of pressures that can have a serious impact on our career paths and how we choose to lead. Instead of the pressure to get a doctorate or climb the corporate ladder, we are pressured to raise a family or remain in more administrative roles. Men don't face those pressures, and it allows them to move up the pay scale faster and fill the C-suite. Dismantling and rebuilding this system can eliminate these pressures and create a more equal vision of what it means to be a "man," a "woman," a "career woman," or anyone that we want to be. All of these expectations and pressures lie in our subconscious minds. The only way to change these beliefs is to acknowledge them, discuss them, and rebuild the system that supported them in the first place.

Maya Humes' Story

When we look at women, we do not automatically assume that they are the person in charge. Women who are standing next to a man are automatically viewed as inferior. We are mistaken as assistants, wives, or employees, rather than a working professional or the CEO. Take an email I received from Maya Humes, a communications professional who has worked on multiple political campaigns over the span of her career. She writes:

> When I was working for one elected official, everyone thought I was his wife or girlfriend. Every single time we were spotted together, and it didn't matter who the person was, they were making that assumption. They thought this despite the fact that I was carrying my work tote bag, was dressed like a staffer, and there was nothing at all to indicate that I was his wife. Also during this same time, elected officials who knew

I wasn't his wife would hit on me shamelessly, even in front of other people. One of them would size me up every time I stood in a circle speaking to him and others, and I could feel his eyes boring into me every time I spoke. He would say things like "You're so cute," and "stop making that face" as though I was trying to seduce him when I never was. All of this made me feel like I was never taken seriously. It reminded me that I was a woman, and reminded me of how few women there are in politics today.

This lie, that women are inferior, can be seen in every single comment that Maya received on the campaign trail. People did not assume that she held roles like chief of staff, communications director, or press secretary. Today, Maya serves as the director of global campaign strategy for the U.S. Department of State. But do people assume this when they look at her? Or are they listening to the lies that they have been told, the lies that insist that the women in the room are inferior, with less prestigious titles, than the men they are working with?

Lorna Little's Story

Even when we have been hired for a position and made great strides in our career, we are underestimated. Our own coworkers do not expect us to rise above the stereotypes placed on us from birth. Lorna Little, the CEO of St. Anne's Family Services, has reflected on moments when these stereotypes cast doubt in the minds of her colleagues. Early in her career, she worked with a behavioral health organization that had an account with a multibillion dollar for-profit company. When the client had their annual meeting in West Palm Beach, Little and the team were invited to join. Little was excited and prepared to meet with the clients, but she could sense that her teammates weren't exactly excited for her to have a seat at the table.

I noticed that the account managers seemed nervous and tense because this was one of our biggest accounts, and I don't think they knew that this young Black woman who came from this urban environment could be more of an asset than a liability.

As the head of the client's company began to ask questions at the dinner table, the managers and directors began to jump in and answer questions. I had no problem with the initial aspect because I can play my position accordingly, but then when he started to ask questions specific to my role, it was clear they were trying to speak for me. Ironically, I knew the responses and some of their responses weren't as clear. He then asked specific questions about the data and my broader thoughts on employee services directly to me. The three people from my agency tried to seem cool but clearly looked nervous. I smiled and answered the questions quoting statistics and trends while being mindful of maintaining confidentiality.

I used my knowledge, my benefit of being able to "see" people and connect with them, and answered the information and the data and provided some analysis. The team smiled. They could take a breath, a sigh of relief. It struck me that they underestimated me and didn't fully take the time to see my full capabilities. I wondered if it was because I was young, or because I was a young Black *woman.*

The team around Little, despite seeing her work for years at the organization, set low expectations for her. Little had earned her place next to everyone at the table, and yet she was still doubted. Fortunately, Little knew how to be an advocate for herself and confidently share her knowledge with her clients, despite their doubts.

Lorna Little has not let the incident she shared remain a memory. She has since turned it into a precautionary tale about setting expectations for others.

I have been careful not to underestimate people within the various organizations I've worked. I take the time to see the diamonds in the rough and provide the opportunity to nurture and develop that talent." Her dream vision for the future of women in leadership? "I hope that women in leadership are seen as the capable and competent leaders we are. I would hope that we continue to support each other, especially in spaces and environments that don't provide the respect and opportunity for growth and success.

In order to reach the vision that Little has for our society, we have to acknowledge the lie that society has been telling us: that women are inferior. This is easier said than done, as we face the consequences of this lie every step of the way.

My Experience at the Transportation Security Administration (TSA)

Remember, this lie is not reality, it is simply a lie that we are told. Women can, do, and will use their education and capabilities to reach the top of the ladder. I have established a successful career as a lawyer, entrepreneur, and media personality. But the lie does not want us to climb this ladder with ease. This lie tells our subconscious mind that women do not belong in the corner office or at the top of the corporate food chain. The system was built for me or any woman to remain inferior. This means that along the way, women recognize extra tasks, inconsiderations, and practices that remind us that the system was not built in our favor. The consequences of this lie *are* a reality.

As I started preparation for post-COVID-19 travel, I made a visit to the TSA office for my TSA PreCheck® classification. I had already completed the online application and was told to show up at the screening appointment with my birth certificate and a valid ID. When I arrived at the facility, I was met with trouble. The man at the office looked at my ID, looked at my birth certificate, and said my documents weren't adequate *because they didn't match.* The TSA website mentioned nothing about bringing a marriage license to the appointment, but the man wouldn't file my paperwork until he saw proof that my name changed due to marriage. He was short with me, even when I explained that there was no reason for me to believe that I needed to bring my marriage license to the screening, as the website mentioned nothing about having a document on hand. He didn't budge.

Fortunately, I live pretty close and had access to my marriage license, but the whole experience disturbed me. The more I thought about it, the more frustrated I became. I graduated from college under my birth name. I graduated from Harvard Law under my birth name. I passed the California State Bar under my birth name. Women might have won awards, earned licenses, built a brand, or written books under their birth name, only to have that erased when they take on a new name.

When I got married, I had to go through the onerous process of changing my registration with the California State Bar. By that time in my life, I had built some equity in that name, and then it was all erased. I spent weeks changing signs on doors and letterheads, stationery, and business cards. I had to get accustomed to that new name. Now, I was facing this process again, years after I was already married.

All women have faced this choice when they get married. Do we want to forgo their "maiden name," a ridiculous term for their birth name, in order to adhere to the system's customs and norms? Or do we want to go against the system? In the 90s, many women hyphenated their name in a sort of compromise to the system. But even then, the process of changing our birth name to a hyphenated name is filled with obstacles and onerous tasks that can last for decades.

In that moment, when I had to dig through my paperwork and find my marriage license, I acknowledged how changing a name is one big bureaucratic step in a system that tells women that we are inferior. We are expected to take on our husband's identity when we are married. We are not expected to have the conflict of keeping a name under which we've accomplished so much. These onerous steps and obstacles all stand on the lie that women are inferior to men.

After the incident with the TSA, I told my daughters never to change their name. Our name means everything in this country. Our name is tied to our profession, to the way we travel, to how we manage money, or even our personal brands. Changing our name doesn't make a relationship stronger or a love deeper, all it does is support the lie that a woman's identity is strengthened by their relationship to a superior man. There's no law that says a male partner can't take on their wife's name. There's no law that says that a woman can't change her name after marriage. My daughters know that the choice to change or keep their name is solely theirs. Avoiding a change can help them avoid all of the steps that fail to consider women in processes like TSA PreCheck® screening.

Inferiority or Imposter Syndrome?

Ignoring or fighting this lie is not an overnight process. The choice to keep your last name after marriage might feel unnatural, even though you know your name is just that— yours. But these are the consequences of a lie that runs deep into our subconscious. The way that we see ourselves and other women have been shaped by this lie. It appears as imposter syndrome, or the doubt that many successful women feel while reflecting on their accomplishments[19]. As you continue on your journey, you have to remind yourself that imposter syndrome is simply supporting the lie that you, and all women, are inferior.

No woman has been able to snap their fingers and remove all of the barriers preventing her from becoming the CEO of a Fortune 500 company. You cannot immediately change a belief or attitude that has been taught and enforced throughout the entirety of a person's life. You alone cannot educate every person in your office on the history of gender discrimination and the privilege that it has afforded men

---

[19] Abigail Abrams, "Yes, Impostor Syndrome Is Real: Here's How to Deal With It," Time (Time, June 20, 2018), https://time.com/5312483/how-to-deal-with-impostor-syndrome/.

for centuries. Identifying and achieving strategies that will rebuild a society without this lie in place will take time. Do not let imposter syndrome tell you that you aren't doing enough!

Along the way, you may experience things like Lorna and I have experienced. You will recognize small tasks and beliefs that support this lie. I'm sure that many people have brushed off the extra documents that women have to bring along with them as "no big deal." But these tasks and obstacles add up. After a while, every small step becomes a never-ending staircase that prevents us from reaching the top. We've got to start building elevators and breaking glass ceilings.

But glass ceilings and cliffs have been cemented into the system over the course of decades, and they are not quick to crumble. You, your sisters, friends, and colleagues will continue to encounter them. On this journey of awakening, you will face pushback from those who are still asleep to gender inequity. You will face misogynistic attitudes. You will face microaggressions that you may decide to ignore for the sake of your larger goals. Imposter syndrome will tell you that you are not good enough, that your dreams are too big, and that you will never see a world where you have the same rights and opportunities as the man next to you. That's false. You are doing exactly what you need to do for yourself, your sisters, and the women who will follow in your footsteps. You may not feel ready for all the shit you have to go through, but trust me. You were built for it. The idea that you are inferior to any man? That's just a lie.

Awakening Action Item. What have you accomplished in the past year? Don't be afraid to congratulate yourself and share what you have done with the world! Write about an accomplishment in your journal and let yourself brag about everything you did to achieve that success. What skills do you possess that made you successful? What sacrifices did you make? Do not let your accomplishments go unnoticed!

CHAPTER 5

The System *Works*— It Just Needs To Be Tweaked

We know, deep inside, that this system needs an overhaul. We know that the expectation to change our name after marriage, the pink tax, and other "normal" customs show how deeply embedded these lies are in our system and society. But the system doesn't want us to know how big the problem is. The final lie that I want to discuss is the lie that the system works—it just needs to be tweaked.

We have been told for *decades* that minor adjustments will bring about the equity that we have been calling for. And I'm not just talking about women. I'm talking about Black women, Black people, the LGBTQ+ community, people with developmental disorders, all groups oppressed by this system. We have all been lied to, thinking we are just one or two steps away from equity. This lie lets us believe that "Band-Aid solutions" will solve the problem, or that we live in a post-racial society due to the end of slavery or segregation. If 2020 has taught us anything, it's that Band-Aid solutions don't work and that progress can easily unravel when the system is built with white supremacist ideals. The system has been built in a way that affects women, women of color, people of color, etc., in a tangled and complicated way. The solution is not to implement one-off solutions, but the system will tell us otherwise.

All of these small solutions, created within the system, uphold the system. We have all found ourselves supporting these Band-Aid solutions now and again, but these are based on a lie. The system doesn't work. It doesn't just need to be tweaked. It needs to be torn down, so that the lies the system tells us do not have to pervade every task, job, and expectation in our everyday lives.

The System's Band-Aid Solutions Didn't Work

The year 2020 will be defined by two major events in our country: the spread of COVID-19 and the murder of George Floyd.

COVID-19 flipped our entire world upside down. Suddenly, Americans faced new questions about where they should go, who they should see, and what activities were considered safe. Guidelines from federal and state governments only added to the confusion. Never in my life would I have imagined going on Facebook Live to talk about a global pandemic. But that's where I was.

As spring turned into summer, our focus was redirected to safety concerns that have *always* been present for Black and Brown people. George Floyd's murder brought the disturbing reality of police brutality to the forefront of our nation's minds. Stories about the global pandemic were replaced by footage of violent protests staged throughout the country. The danger of COVID-19 was briefly forgotten or minimized by the dangers of tear gas and rubber bullets. City officials began to seriously debate police budgets and whether it was time to defund the police. The horrific murders of George Floyd and Breonna Taylor called for serious conversations on what it means to be Black in America.

Discussions on race and policing obviously must take place at different times than discussions on empowering women in business. I'm not going to spend much time talking about how we can minimize violence by law enforcement. The parallels between these two issues, however, provide a clear path to untangling the disenfranchisement experienced by Black people *and* women in America. The system, as a response, hands us this lie: that small solutions, that women and Black people must implement, will result in the end of their oppression. But when Band-Aid solutions do not work and the system continues to hold us down, we are left with the blame. Band-Aid solutions have never been the answer, but the lie tells us otherwise. As women, as Black people, as a country, we need to think and act on a larger scale. Only then will we see changes that allow all people to live in an equitable, just world.

The System Will Repeat History

When I started getting calls to comment on issues of race and policing in America, I felt like I was experiencing déjà vu. I had to ask myself: was I in 2020, or did I travel back in time to 1992? 2012? 2014? Black Lives Matter was formed in 2012. Chants of "No Justice, No Peace," did not begin with the death of George Floyd. Hashtags like #SayTheirNames have shone a spotlight on race and policing for years. Protests highlighting systemic racism within law enforcement have been happening for *decades*. Why is our country facing a violent and horrific Groundhog Day, and when will it stop?

I really thought we had reached a turning point six years prior. In 2014, the murders of Michael Brown and Eric Garner sparked protests throughout the country. Things felt "different" than they had at protests following Trayvon Martin's murder two years earlier. Black Lives Matter was a national movement. By the end of the year, the Federal Bureau of Investigation (FBI) began to officially track fatal police shootings. Body cameras were becoming a popular bipartisan solution. Real changes were made and real conversations were had on national platforms. I remember the hope that these changes brought me in 2014. Friends, family members, and colleagues believed we would see a significant decline in fatal shootings by police—but we were wrong. We believed the lie that this solution would help to curb racially-based police brutality in America.

Six years later, although Black Lives Matter *protests* resemble the protests surrounding Michael Brown, Eric

Garner, or Trayvon Martin's deaths, the calls for action were different. In 2014, the calls to defund or abolish the police were not as popular as they have been in 2020. In 2014, more radical demands were pushed aside to make way for moderate, actionable tweaks to the system. These tweaks included the tracking of fatal police shootings and initiatives to include more de-escalation training in local police departments. Body cameras, in particular, became the star of the show.

Body camera footage aimed to take the "he said, he said" out of police shootings. If a police officer knew that their every move would be recorded, would they still be willing to shoot at an unarmed person? Would they use racially-charged language? Could higher-ups (and the American people) hold every police officer accountable for leaving children fatherless, mothers grieving, and communities hurting?

In 2014, the answer was "yes." Legislators, law enforcement, and Americans calling for justice believed that body cameras would bring change. The next year, 95 percent of police departments (at the federal, state, and local level) vowed to start using body cameras. (Only 19 percent claimed that their body camera programs were "fully operational" at the time[20].) The next year, federal legislators gave police departments over $40 million in grants to equip their officers with cameras[21]. We had won. Change was on the horizon. Or was it?

---

[20] Lafayette Group, "Technology Needs - Body Worn Cameras" (Homeland Security Office of Emergency Communications, December 2015), https://assets.bwbx.io/documents/users/iqjWHBFdfxIU/rvnT.EAJQwK4/v0.

[21] Amanda Ripley and Timothy Williams, "Body Cameras Have Little Effect on Police Behavior, Study Says," Body Cameras Have Little Effect on Police Behavior, Study Says | The New York Times (The New York Times Company, October 21, 2017), https://www.nytimes.com/2017/10/20/us/police-body-camera-study.html.

Body Cameras Don't Work

It has been over five years since 95 percent of police departments vowed to put body cameras on officers. Over 5,000 people have been shot and killed by the police. Black people still continue to be shot at disproportionate rates. Black mothers watch their children leave the house *every day* wondering, "Will they be next?" Brilliant and innocent citizens are robbed of their rights to life, liberty, and the pursuit of happiness. And although body cameras have made *some* positive changes, experts say that this strategy is not the solution that it promised to be.

Why have body cameras failed to prevent the deaths of over 5,000 people who were shot by police? Experts do not have just one answer. Some answers are simple: officers wearing body cameras choose not to turn them on. This was the case during David McAtee's death. McAtee was killed on June 1, 2020, by members of the Kentucky National Guard who were assisting the Louisville Metro Police Department in their attempts to disperse demonstrators protesting police brutality. Details of the altercation involving McAtee were lacking because police chose to leave their body cameras off. This is the same department that was responsible for the death of twenty-six-year-old emergency room technician Breonna Taylor. Initial reports claimed that officers at the scene didn't have to turn on body cameras before the raid on Taylor's home, nor were they required to wear them in the first place.

Even when body camera footage is collected, it is not always reviewed or released to the public. Outrage over George Floyd's murder began *months* before body camera footage was released to the public. Cell phone videos and security camera footage were shared on social media immediately. Body camera footage was still being released over three months *after* Floyd's murder[22]. In clear-cut cases

---

[22] Brakkton Booker, "Body Camera Video Of George Floyd And Police Offers New Details Of Deadly Encounter," New Bodycam Footage Released From George Floyd Killing (NPR, August 14, 2020), https://www.npr.org/sections/live-updates-protests-for-racial-

with video evidence like George Floyd's, justice is still not guaranteed. The Minneapolis Police Department fired the officers involved a day after Floyd's murder, but the first officer was not formally charged (with third-degree murder and second-degree manslaughter) until four days later. The other three officers in the video were charged with aiding and abetting the murder on June 3[23]. If officers are not fired or formally charged, they are protected by policies like qualified immunity. Why does it feel like we've made no progress between 2014 and 2020?

Body camera footage or other solutions enacted six years ago did not stop the murders of George Floyd, Breonna Taylor, David McAtee, or hundreds of other Black and Brown people murdered by police brutality. When we look at these "solutions" now, we see that they are merely Band-Aids. Band-Aids may provide protection in the short term, but they do not prevent people from getting wounded again and again. People calling for justice are no longer willing to accept "Band-Aids" or tweaks to the system anymore. Advocates are thinking bigger and looking to more whole-scale solutions. Body cameras are a solution within this system, and the system continues to feed us lies and hold us down.

In order to truly prevent senseless deaths like that of Breonna Taylor, we need to address the *lies* that built this system and allow these deaths to happen without consequences. We also need to make sweeping systemic changes. Similarly, in order to reach gender equity in the workplace and larger society, we need to address the system that allows harassment, pay gaps, and other acts to happen without consequences. Racism and sexism are entwined with the systems in which our very country is built. The only

---

justice/2020/08/14/902539820/body-camera-video-of-george-floyd-and-police-offers-new-details-of-deadly-encoun.

[23] Derrick Bryson Taylor, "George Floyd Protests: A Timeline," A Timeline of the George Floyd Protests - The New York Times (The New York Times Company, May 30, 2020), https://www.nytimes.com/article/george-floyd-protests-timeline.html.

path toward true equity is dismantling these systems and rebuilding them.

I say this as a proud American who appreciates the freedoms that we are given in this country. I love America, and *because* I love it, I'm not afraid or unwilling to challenge systemic racism and sexism within the country. The system is deeply flawed, and we cannot be afraid to address the lies that it has told us since the founding of this country. But we're not here just to tear the system down. Together, we can rebuild the country from the ground up and provide equity and opportunity to all people. We can remove the lies from the equation altogether.

The System Will Tell You It's Not Your Problem

Despite the spin that many people place on groups like Black Lives Matter, the issue of race and policing is not just one of Black vs. white. Every single person is affected by systemic racism: white, Black, Brown, young, old, Republican, Democrat, etc. Certainly, people of privilege have a lot more to learn than people who are the targets of racism and prejudice every single day. But just because you or someone who looks like you have *experienced* violent acts of systemic racism does *not* mean you are immune from holding onto the ideals or supporting organizations that support that system.

None of this is new to Black people. We experience prejudice, racism, and violence caused by the system every single day. Black children are taught to obey and fear police in ways that white children never needed to learn. Our families, friends, and colleagues in the Black community have conversations on race that may shock and amaze white people who do not experience racism on a daily basis.

But these conversations may not be enough. If conversations on race and policing does not leave the dinner table of a Black family's home, or a roundtable featuring solely Black lecturers, organizers, and audience members, we will not get very far. If camera footage of George Floyd or of protests in Portland stayed in individuals' camera rolls, we would not get very far. People supporting the Black Lives Matter movement are at the head of this fight against police brutality and systemic racism, but we cannot dismantle a centuries-old system on our own. People with privilege, people who are white, people at "the top" have to take action, too. They cannot take proper action until they have context about systemic racism. At the same time, men in C-suites and holding political office cannot take proper action to promote gender equity until they have context about sexism in the workplace, home, or government.

At the end of the day, Breonna Taylor's murderers were not charged with her death because officers and authorities in Louisville failed to hold them accountable. Brett Hankison was fired on June 23, over three months *after* Breonna Taylor was killed. He was not charged for the death of Breonna Taylor; he was only charged for "wanton endangerment" after authorities claimed that he put Taylor's *neighbors* in danger[24]. The two other officers at the scene (Jonathan Mattingly and Myles Cosgrove) were not arrested alongside Hankison. They were placed on paid administrative leave and not charged with a single crime. (This means that they are not required to work, but are still getting paid a salary.) The Kentucky attorney general failed to meet with Taylor's family until August, five months after she had been killed[25].

These are decisions that can *solely* be made by the attorney general and people within the Louisville Police Department. I do not have the authority to charge the police officers who killed Breonna Taylor, or the police officers

---

[24] Marisa Iati et al., "Officer Brett Hankison Charged with Wanton Endangerment; Two Officers Shot during Protests," The Washington Post (WP Company, September 25, 2020), https://www.washingtonpost.com/nation/2020/09/23/breonna-taylor-charging-decision/.

[25] Eric Levenson and Elizabeth Joseph, "Kentucky Attorney General Met Breonna Taylor's Family for the First Time, over 150 Days after Her Death," CNN (Cable News Network, August 13, 2020), https://www.cnn.com/2020/08/13/us/breonna-taylor-louisville-police/index.html.

who killed *anyone* in the past five years, with murder. Most likely, you do not have that authority, either. If we want to see systemic change, we need to reach the people who have the authority to make those changes. We need to reach decision-makers. We need to reach people who are *already* in power, who can give people the *opportunity* to be in power themselves.

Again, this message is not exclusive to racial injustice. Black people, people of color, women of color, women, women with disabilities, people with disabilities—we cannot rely on Band-Aid solutions anymore. We need to see larger changes. If we want to see systemic change, we need to reach the people who have the authority to make those changes. The *system* is flawed. In order to see the change that we want to see, we need to make changes to the *system*. We need to reach the people who have control within the system.

This may be frustrating to hear. The people in charge of investigating Breonna Taylor's murder (including members of the FBI) may feel inaccessible. A better representation of women in government and leadership positions may feel inaccessible. This is why we keep fighting, keep protesting, and keep calling our representatives. We need people in law enforcement to accomplish the goals set by activists and victims of systemic racism. Similarly, we need people in boardrooms to make decisions that will undo the work of systemic sexism. The conversation about inequity and injustice *needs* to leave the dinner table and needs to acknowledge the lies that we have been told.

The System Needs an Overhaul

Band-Aid solutions have not prevented Black people from getting shot and killed by police. Band-Aid solutions have not given women equal access to the C-suite or equal pay. We need large-scale change. We need to listen to the people who are calling to defund or abolish police systems, reimagine gender roles, and dismantle the system for good. The system needs an overhaul.

Sexism runs rampant in the boardroom, in the bedroom, and in every element of our lives. These lies continue to enforce this divide, and you may even hold onto beliefs or expectations that support this system. Only when we recognize the need for (and implement) large-scale change can we begin to move toward a world with gender equity, income equity, and a more fair world for all.

What Band-Aid solutions have women used to try and earn equal pay? What do large-scale solutions look like? These are two of the questions that I will continue to address. Learning from past mistakes and looking to the future is a responsibility that you, I, our partners, our colleagues, and our friends must take up to see a more equal and equitable world. Together, we can awaken ourselves and fight back against the system.

I am writing this book as a woman who has seen first-hand the obstacles that working women face every day. Over the course of my career, I have been knocked down. People have doubted me. I was tricked into thinking that hard work was the *only* thing that I, or any woman across the country, needed to achieve success. I believed that my beauty contributed to my worth and that one day I might have to make a choice between my children and my career. I upheld and believed the lies that supported the oppression of women—but no more.

As I acknowledged the lies we have been told and the harsh realities of inequity among women, I carried on. When I was knocked down, I got up. When I was denied the path reserved for more privileged women, I forged my own. You, too, have the ability to navigate your industry and reach your goals despite a system determined to hold you down. As you awaken and rise past the obstacles within this system, you can use your power and influence to help women throughout society reach their goals, too.

Band-Aid solutions do not work because they do not aim to help *every* woman who wants success. They neglect women with children, women with unsupportive partners, or women who were not born with copious amounts of money. Hard work is not the only thing that a woman (or person) needs to achieve success. Connections, advocates, and monetary resources will put you farther ahead than anyone without them. Women can work themselves to the bone, but if men at the top of the company deny them access to the C-suite, women will remain vastly underrepresented. We are *all* responsible for large-scale change. Band-Aid solutions have attempted to untangle sexism in the workplace, but you can take the first steps in dismantling and rebuilding a system currently plagued with sexist ideals. We are *all* responsible for bringing big changes to the way that women are represented in business, in government, and in the country. We *all* can stop spreading the lies that the system has told us.

Dismantle the System

Not everyone is going to accept or be willing to undergo the unlearning process immediately. Unraveling the lies that you have been told about the world is a painful, frustrating, and scary process. Cognitive dissonance, or holding onto contradictory beliefs, values, or ideas , is instinctually something that the human mind wants to avoid. We want simplicity. We want to believe that the world is equal. We do not want to believe that our teachers, parents, or friends may have lied to us about the treatment and status of women in this country.

As an African-American woman, I have seen friends endure the struggle to unlearn the reality of racial inequity. The murders of George Floyd, Michael Brown, and Breonna Taylor served as an "awakening" for white people who believed we lived in a post-racial country. The Trump Administration refused to acknowledge that racism exists in America. We know the harm in ignorance like this every time the Black Lives Matter movement is brought up in the media. When people fail to acknowledge racial inequity, they fail to understand the calls for justice and the devastation that African-Americans feel every day that justice is not served and the dehumanization of African-Americans continues.

African-Americans must also undergo their own unlearning process. I am not immune to lessons crafted and distributed by systemic racism. Similarly, women must get in the habit of looking at the system with a critical eye. Why do we feel the pressure to stay at home when our male partner is perfectly capable of taking on more childcare duties? Who should be the person to determine whether a male or female colleague deserves higher pay? When did we learn what was a "man's job" and what was "women's work?"

Let's explore these issues further.

Awakening Action Item. Take out your journal and dream of a world without systemic sexism or racism. What would it look like? What would it *not* look like? Identify the current systems that need to be dismantled before this ideal world can be built.

SECTION 2

Exploring The Problem

CHAPTER 6

How Did We Get Here?

The lies that we have been told *have* been addressed in previous chapters, but there is one problem that we must explore. Previous moments and media, from Sheryl Sandberg's and Nell Scovell's *Lean In* to the #MeToo movement to calling out prejudiced behavior on social media, have largely failed to consider the struggles of all women. They assume that *we* as women are not doing enough to fight for gender equity. As we explore the lies that we have been told and the solutions that we have tried to implement, we must address one question: how did we get here?

Lean In

Let's hop into our mental time machines for a minute and go back to 2013. Forget the #MeToo movement, forget TikTok, forget COVID-19. The Equal Pay Act celebrated its 50th birthday in 2013, but women in corporate positions knew that wage disparities were still in place.

Sheryl Sandberg, COO of Facebook, had already given a TED Talk on this issue. "Why We Have Too Few Women Leaders" is cited as the catalyst for the *Lean In* movement. It has been viewed over ten million times. By the time Sandberg published *Lean In* in 2013, she had amassed a following that was ready to accelerate their careers and demand the life that they wanted. *Lean In* soared to the top of the Amazon Best-Sellers list on the day that it was released, and made the top of *The New York Times*' Best-Seller list within two weeks and stayed for over a year. The book has sold over 4.2 million copies[26].

Although the book gained immense praise from women and men who were already hooked by Sandberg's message, not everyone was excited to *Lean In*. For every review praising the book's life-changing messages, another review picked it apart and asked for more. Why is this book so controversial? Sandberg wants to see women succeeding and earning as much as their male counterparts. Critics argued that the assumptions that Sandberg makes throughout the book, however, may fail to consider the efforts, actions, and attitudes of women throughout history.

Other critics praised the importance of the book, but refused to pretend that it was applicable to every woman. Janet Maslin (literary critic for *The New York Times*) wrote, "[*Lean In*] will open the eyes of women who grew up thinking that feminism was ancient history, who recoil at the word but walk heedlessly through the doors it opened. And it will encourage those women to persevere in their professional lives, even if Ms. Sandberg's own domestic and career balance sounds like something out of a fairy tale[27]."

In 2013, Sandberg's calls to push through a woman's inclinations toward passivity and demand for men to tidy around the house appeared to be the conclusion of a fairy tale. Years later, women do not live happily ever after. We still have many issues to put on the table before we could begin to talk about equity in the workplace. We still have many issues to put on the table before we can shut the book on inequity and inequality and live in the fairy tale that we want to promise the next generation of girls.

---

[26] Judith Newman, "'Lean In': Five Years Later," The New York Times (The New York Times Company, March 16, 2018), https://www.nytimes.com/2018/03/16/business/lean-in-five-years-later.html#:~:text=It%20rode%20the%20New%20York,all%20formats)%2C%20landed%20Ms.

[27] Janet Maslin, "Lessons From the Stratosphere, and How to Get There," Sheryl Sandberg's 'Lean In' Offers Lessons - The New York Times (The New York Times Company, March 6, 2013), https://www.nytimes.com/2013/03/07/books/sheryl-sandbergs-lean-in.html.

Do not take these critiques as a smear campaign against Sheryl Sandberg. In recent years, events like #MeToo and Sandberg's personal journey has led *her* to rethink some of the assumptions and arguments made in *Lean In*. But, as the book continues to be the subject of think pieces and a guide for women to "get ahead" in their careers, I think examining the flaws of this book is important to understanding why traditional career advice for women may not produce the results that we want.

There are some big problems that came out of the past decade's proposed solutions to sexism in the workplace. If we want women to succeed, we need to consider all women: poor women, women without partners, women who are disabled, etc. We also need to include men in discussions about pay disparity and how systemic sexism is around the workplace. But let's not get ahead of ourselves.

Lean In's critics are not just disgruntled men who want women to stay at home and watch the children. The book has received criticism and skepticism from women including bell hooks, who called the book a piece of "faux feminism[28]." Michelle Obama even referenced the book at a *Becoming* tour stop, saying "And it's not always enough to lean in, because that shit doesn't work all the time[29]."

Make Your Partner a "Real" Partner

The title of one chapter, "Make your Partner a Real Partner" already fails a large group of professional women: single mothers. Sandberg's solution within this chapter is to simply ask your partner to do more around the house. Women

[28] bell hooks, "Dig Deep: Beyond Lean In," Dig Deep: Beyond Lean In - The Feminist Wire (The Feminist Wire, October 28, 2013), https://thefeministwire.com/2013/10/17973/.

[29] Aja Romano, "Michelle Obama on Sheryl Sandberg's Lean In Philosophy: 'That Shit Doesn't Work All the Time!'," Michelle Obama on Sheryl Sandberg's Lean In philosophy: "That shit doesn't work all the time!" (Vox Media, December 3, 2018), https://www.vox.com/culture/2018/12/3/18123796/michelle-obama-criticizes-lean-in-becoming-tour.

without partners simply cannot access this solution, but women with partners don't find this to be so easy, either.

Simply put, our society continues to value men's work over women's work. Asking your husband (provided that you have one) to take on more chores and childcare responsibilities does not change the fact that the extra work you can put into your career will not be valued as much as the work a man puts into his career. A shared earning/ shared parenting marriage among a straight or LGBTQ+ couple will not change how a woman's work is viewed by her male counterparts. A chore chart or diaper duty for husbands is a Band-Aid. We need large-scale change.

Our mothers and grandmothers were alive in a time when women were solely expected to be homemakers. Recent progress, although celebrated, hasn't been quite as progressive as early advocates might have envisioned. Now, women are simply expected to be the breadwinner *and* the homemaker. Single moms and women with economic hardships still find themselves looking for an extra hour or two in the day—or better yet, a job that recognizes how much they have on their plate.

Sandberg herself has admitted that the chapter failed to address the struggles and expectations of single moms. In 2015, Sandberg lost her husband, Dave. The next year, she wrote a Mother's Day post on Facebook reflecting on her experiences:

> In *Lean In*, I emphasized how critical a loving and supportive partner can be for women both professionally and personally—and how important Dave was to my career and to our children's development. I still believe this. Some people felt that I did not spend enough time writing about the difficulties women face when they have an unsupportive partner or no partner at all. They were right.
>
> I will never experience and understand all of the challenges most single moms face, but I understand a lot more than I did a year ago. Our widespread

cultural assumption that every child lives with a two-parent heterosexual married couple is out of date. Since the early 1970s, the number of single mothers in the United States has nearly doubled. Today, almost 30 percent of families with children are headed by a single parent, and 84 percent of those are led by a single mother. And yet our attitudes and our policies do not reflect this shift.

Single moms have been leaning in for a long time—out of necessity and a desire to provide the best possible opportunities for their children[30].

The "Howard/Heidi" Stereotype

Another example of this bias is the "Howard/Heidi" stereotype. In *Lean In,* Sandberg cites a study in which some participants were asked to read the story of Heidi Roizen, a successful Venture Capitalist (VC). Other participants read the same story, but the protagonist's name was changed to Howard Roizen. After reading, participants gave their impressions of Howard/Heidi. The study shows how successful men tend to be perceived as go-getters and likeable, while successful women are immediately put down as selfish or unlikeable.

Sandberg speaks directly to women about what we can do to overcome the stereotypes and biases that hold women down. Rather, I should say that Sandberg speaks directly to women about what *more* we can do to overcome stereotypes. Do women really need to add "change our personality to become more likeable" onto our to-do lists?

Susan Adams, senior editor in charge of *Forbes'* education coverage, says: "The problem is not that women are leaning into their identity as Heidi. Even if women skirted around the Howard/Heidi results completely, the results of

---

[30] Emily Crockett, "How the Death of Sheryl Sandberg's Husband Made Her Rethink Lean In," How the death of Sheryl Sandberg's husband made her rethink Lean In (Vox Media, May 9, 2016), https://www.vox.com/2016/5/9/11640052/sheryl-sandberg-lean-in-husbands-death-single-mom-facebook.

the study would still be the same. There would still be men and women who relied on biases and ignorance and make the same assessments about Howard and Heidi[31]."

Instead of telling women that they are "wrong" for leaning into Heidi, we need to address why the Howard/Heidi stereotypes exist in the first place. People need to recognize how they have relied on these stereotypes in the past. Women, as well as men, participated in the Howard/Heidi stereotype. Instead of relying on women alone to *lean into* Howard, we must all find ways to tackle the larger problem of the stereotype's existence. The expectations of what it means to be a man or woman at work do not solely exist in the office. Together, we must all "zoom out" and change the system that puts these expectations in place.

On a similar note, *Lean In* consistently tells women that they are the reason behind pay inequity. If only *we* asked for more, left our children at daycare, and cut our household duties in half, we too could navigate the corporate jungle gym. *We,* as women, have not been doing enough, although *we* cannot have it all in the first place.

Sandberg has stepped back from some of the claims that she makes in *Lean In*. Hindsight is certainly 20/20, but the passage of time is not the only factor that has prevented *Lean In* from being the manifesto that many claimed it could be after its release. In this new decade, we must ask ourselves how far women have come since the movement began, and what we need to do to move forward and dismantle a system of sexism that is undeniably still present in the workforce and society at large.

Change Isn't Going to Happen Overnight

Lean In helped to place wage disparity under a national spotlight and kicked off many important conversations about diversity,

---

[31] Susan Adams, "10 Things Sheryl Sandberg Gets Exactly Right In 'Lean In'," 10 Things Sheryl Sandberg Gets Exactly Right In 'Lean In' (Forbes Magazine, March 4, 2013), https://www.forbes.com/sites/susanadams/2013/03/04/10-things-sheryl-sandberg-gets-exactly-right-in-lean-in/#18b0929b7ada.

equity, and sexism. The years that followed its publication show not only how *dire* these conversations are, but also what these conversations have been missing. Sandberg wrote from a privileged perspective, one that she has started to truly see as time goes on. The failure to recognize some of her privileges is not a reason to discredit her, but simply a reason to take a step back and look at the *entire* picture.

When we look at the struggles of women in the workplace, we cannot simply look at a woman's motivation or pressure to "be likeable." We must consider the lies that are told to *every* child from the moment (or before) they are born. Band-Aids don't work when we are fighting off policies, stereotypes, and expectations that hurt women on a larger scale. Larger solutions that address systemic sexism are needed to make any real progress.

The Power of Social Media: #BlackLivesMatter, #MeToo, and Others

Women who use social media do not have to wait around for another author to advocate for them. Platforms like Twitter, Instagram, and Facebook have given women of all professions a platform in which they can advocate for themselves. Through content production and smart social media strategy, women can show off their strengths, develop a following, and connect with people who can help them get ahead.

This is a central idea in my book *Make It Rain*. Social media has been a powerful influence in achieving large-scale wins: dismantling systemic sexism, racism, and other power struggles. The accessibility of social media can also reveal the lies that we have been told faster than critics can comment on books or other forms of literature.

#BlackLivesMatter

Is there a better example of the power of social media in the fight against oppression than #BlackLivesMatter? The first usage of #BlackLivesMatter as a hashtag occurred in 2013, when Black Lives Matter (BLM) co-founder Alicia Garza used it to respond to Trayvon Martin's death. It has since morphed into an international rallying cry for racial justice and reform, alongside being an actual organization that fights for these changes. Unless you have been on "Do Not Disturb" mode for the past eight or so years, you have probably signed a petition, learned about a candidate, or shared information related to #BlackLivesMatter through social media.

#BlackLivesMatter made its mark, but the power of this hashtag is especially apparent in 2021 and beyond. In the thirty days following the death of George Floyd, #BlackLivesMatter was used on social media *eighty million* times. (On May 28, #BlackLivesMatter was used on social media over eight million times. To compare, use of the term #Starbucks was used less than 45,000 times[32].) Data also shows that the protests following George Floyd's death were searched more than any other type of protest in history. The changes made to curb police brutality and dismantle systemic racism far exceeded the changes made during other resurgences of the #BlackLivesMatter movement. It is hard to reflect on the overwhelming social media content related to the deaths of George Floyd and *not* credit social media for spreading awareness and advocating for change.

#MeToo

A similar hashtag, #MeToo, brought awareness to not only the accusations against Harvey Weinstein, American film producer, but the "Me Too" movement itself. In 2006, Tarana Burke was the first woman to use the "Me Too" phrase as a way of supporting women of color who were survivors of sexual abuse. The campaign gained national attention when Alyssa Milano used the hashtag #MeToo to speak out against

---

[32] Brittany Levine Beckman, "#BlackLivesMatter Saw Tremendous Growth on Social Media. Now What?," Black Lives Matter, George Floyd dominated social media. Now what? (Mashable, Inc., July 2, 2020), https://mashable.com/article/black-lives-matter-george-floyd-social-media-data/.

Harvey Weinstein and encourage other women to share their experiences with sexual harassment and abuse. Shortly after, Burke took to Twitter to reclaim her contributions to the movement and spread awareness about her campaign.

Social media served two important purposes in the 2017 resurgence of the #MeToo movement. The first purpose was spreading awareness about how sexual misconduct impacted women throughout the globe, from famous actresses to the "everyday woman." The second purpose was to provide accurate information that kept gatekeepers in check. If Burke had not spoken out about her place in the #MeToo movement, her work may have been misappropriated by Milano's social media following. Burke had not envisioned her campaign to become a rallying cry for women around the world—when she first saw the hashtag trending, she thought, "Social media is not a safe space...this is going to be a fucking disaster[33]." Burke isn't totally wrong. She was seeing her words, which had not received much attention eleven years earlier, finally gain a measure of notoriety when they were used by a white woman. This, once again, shows how deep and intersectional the lies that we have been told run. The system isn't just oppressing women equally. Women of color, disabled women, and LGBTQ+ women face additional struggles, from being gaslit to being plagiarized to simply being ignored. As we reflect on this movement and other recent movements addressing the lies that we have been told, we must remember to keep our solutions intersectional and consider *all* women.

My #MeToo Story

Social media moves fast, and the lies that we have been told barge their way into the conversation fast, too. In 2017, I went on a CNN morning show to comment on the

---

[33] Emma Brocks, "#MeToo Founder Tarana Burke: 'You Have to Use Your Privilege to Serve Other People'," #MeToo founder Tarana Burke: 'You have to use your privilege to serve other people' (Guardian News and Media, January 15, 2018), https://www.theguardian.com/world/2018/jan/15/me-too-founder-tarana-burke-women-sexual-assault.

#MeToo movement and Harvey Weinstein sexual assault case. After the appearance, I received a frustratingly and almost comically ironic email from a viewer: "Dear Ms. Martin, I would respectfully suggest that your attire for these interviews, especially on this topic, should be more modest... This morning on CNN you had on a top or dress that revealed substantial cleavage, which some, who would wrongly discount your message, [would say] serves to further objectify women[34]."

Instead of deleting the email and moving on, I wrote an op-ed piece as a response. I couldn't just ignore the misogyny (and irony) within that statement. This man was watching me have a conversation about holding women to a different standard, and decided that I must continue to be held to a different standard. If he had been listening to what I was saying, he might have taken a step back and examined his judgement. He didn't. He took time out of his busy life to find my email and write to me.

This was one of many exhausting incidents that defined the #MeToo movement and discussions about sexual harassment in the workplace. If you worked in a corporate setting during this time, you probably have a list of incidents like this sitting in the back of your brain. Women at the forefront of the #MeToo movement showed laudable bravery as they shared their stories of sexual assault, misconduct, and harassment. Rather than *leaning in* to support women and lift them up, many men found themselves backing away due to fears of allegations.

This response shows one of the largest problems of relying on women to solely enact change. The #MeToo movement and other attempts to reach solutions to sexism also shows how tangled the web of lies and systemic sexism can be. We cannot pretend that every woman, mother, or professional experiences the same type of discrimination or obstacles as the woman next to her. And as we consider

[34] Areva Martin, "How I Got Slut-Shamed After My TV Interview on Sexual Harassment," I Was Slut-Shamed While Talking About Sexual Harassment (Time, December 8, 2017), https://time.com/5054213/slut-shaming-sexual-harassment/.

ableism, the LGBTQ+ community, and single mothers, we must also consider what goes on in *and* outside the office. Lies told outside of the workplace often affect what goes on *inside* the workplace. Unless people across the board are willing to acknowledge their privilege, and take the time to untangle the web within systemic sexism, we cannot fully eradicate the lies that continue to be spread about gender equity.

Using Social Media to Get Around Human Resource (HR) Departments

As time goes on, we are seeing more examples of how social media can influence change on a large scale. The right voices and strategy can also illuminate microaggressions and problems within individual organizations. By highlighting the wrongdoing of business leaders or corporations, we can continue the conversation on sexism, racism, and other forms of discrimination.

Social media becomes a way of advocating for change when HR departments or business leaders refuse to acknowledge problems in the workplace. Examples of this strategy include the complaints made against leaders at Refinery29, *The Ellen DeGeneres Show*, and many other companies that appear (on the outside) to be forward-thinking.

These complaints, ironically, often begin when brands try to express solidarity with movements like #MeToo or #BlackLivesMatter. On June 2, 2020, Ashley Alese Edwards, a former director at Refinery29 tweeted, "Hey @Refinery29, cool blacked out homepage! But you know what real allyship looks like? Paying your Black employees fairly, having Black women in top leadership positions & addressing the microaggressions your Black employees deal with from management on a daily basis." Other employees and former employees started to step forward and share their stories of discrimination, pay disparity, and tokenization. The writers stepping forward used their own hashtag, #BlackatR29, to come forward and share their stories.

Within a week, the top editor and co-founder of the company stepped down.

Refinery29's controversy made national news in the midst of the controversy surrounding *The Ellen DeGeneres Show*. In March of 2020, comedy writer Kevin T. Porter took to Twitter and asked for "the most insane stories you've heard about Ellen being mean" in exchange for a $2 donation to the L.A. Food Bank. Porter received thousands of responses from former employees and people who had worked with or around Ellen. Allegations ranged, but focused primarily on the show's toxic workplace environment and harassment from Ellen and her staff. The thread that followed Porter's tweet was picked up by news outlets, and more sources began to report on the allegations against the show. Additional hashtags and news coverage continued to make headlines. By July, WarnerMedia had announced that they were conducting an internal investigation into the company's culture.

The Ellen DeGeneres Show was not under investigation because of the complaints made to HR, but because of people talking about the complaints online. And this show is not alone. The CEO of *ESSENCE* magazine stepped down in June after allegations of abusive workplace behavior surfaced on social media. A CEO at a Boston-based bakery stepped down after employees shared an online petition for her resignation. The editor-in-chief of *Bon Appétit* resigned after photos of him in brownface made their rounds on social media alongside accusations of discrimination and huge pay disparities among creators of color.

What we're seeing is a moment of reckoning. Social media is a powerful tool. A simple airing of grievances online can draw attention to a company in ways that internal HR complaints could never do. Sponsors pull their support. Creators vow not to contribute to toxic companies and consumers vow to take their money elsewhere. CEOs resign. These tangible changes show how drastic and fast social media works compared to traditional media. Whether you are a CEO, an entrepreneur, or someone who is looking to share a message with others, social media can help you advocate for yourself.

Where Are We Now?

We cannot pretend that 2013 was the beginning and end of women's fight for pay equity. If the last decade has taught us anything, it is that not all movements or solutions will bring us the results we want if sexism is still ingrained in our system. Women continue to hit walls held up by a foundation that needs to be dismantled.

We have made some progress since 2013. We saw the first woman and woman of color run for president and vice president, respectively, backed by a major political party. The number of female CEOs for Fortune 500 companies jumped from twenty in 2013 to thirty-seven in 2020[35]. Mary Winston became the second Black woman *ever* to be named the CEO of a Fortune 500 company. (She acted as interim CEO of Bed, Bath & Beyond and was replaced by Mark J. Tritton less than seven months later[36].) Women started to ask for more money and the pay gap has been narrowing (slightly[37]). National conversations about sexual harassment in the workplace, equal pay, and general job discrimination have brought attention to these issues.

---

[35] Emma Hinchliffe, "The Number of Women Running Fortune 500 Companies Hits an All-Time Record," Fortune 500 CEOs who are women hits record high | Fortune (Fortune Media IP Limited, May 20, 2020), https://fortune.com/2020/05/18/women-ceos-fortune-500-2020/.

[36] "Bed Bath & Beyond Inc. Names Mark J. Tritton as President and Chief Executive Officer," Bed Bath & Beyond Inc. Names Mark J. Tritton as President and Chief Executive Officer (Bed Bath & Beyond Inc., October 9, 2019), https://www.prnewswire.com/news-releases/bed-bath--beyond-inc-names-mark-j-tritton-as-president-and-chief-executive-officer-300935010.html.

[37] Kathy Gurchiek, "Study: Global Gender Pay Gap Has Narrowed but Still Exists," Study: Global Gender Pay Gap Has Narrowed but Still Exists (SHRM, March 24, 2021), https://www.shrm.org/resourcesandtools/hr-topics/behavioral-competencies/global-and-cultural-effectiveness/pages/study-gender-pay-gap-narrows-but-still-exists.aspx.

Like the election of President Barack Obama in 2008, the nomination of Hillary Clinton or the election of Kamala Harris are not signs that we are past sexism in society. Individual cases and changes in data do not prove that people are still taught, in subtle and not-so-subtle ways, that men are superior to women, that they're smarter than women, that they are more capable than women, that they're greater than women. Data on women in C-suite roles does not reflect the pressure that is put on each woman to balance the desire to be breadwinner *and* homemaker.

People have even *pushed back* on the progress that women have made to achieve equal pay. The gender pay gap has widened in the tech industry[38]. When comparing two soccer seasons containing twenty exhibition wins, male players would make $13,166 per game compared to female players' $4,950 salary per game[39]. In 2019, a federal judge dismissed a case that claimed there was a pay disparity within the U.S. Soccer Federation. Many experts *continue* to neglect the different pay disparities when it comes to race. Leaders celebrate that women now earn eighty-two cents to a white man's dollar, but fail to acknowledge that Black women only make sixty-three cents to that same dollar[40].

---

[38] Nina Zipkin, "These Female Entrepreneurs Created a Fake Male Co-Founder to Work Around Sexism. How Well It Worked Is Incredibly Eye Opening.," These Female Entrepreneurs Created a Fake Male Co-Founder to Work Around Sexism. How Well It Worked Is Incredibly Eye Opening. (Entrepreneur Media Inc., September 1, 2017), https://www.entrepreneur.com/article/299649.

[39] Seth Vertelney, "USWNT Players Sue U.S. Soccer for Gender Discrimination," USWNT lawsuit: 28 players sue U.S. Soccer for gender discrimination | Goal.com (Goal.com, March 8, 2019), https://www.goal.com/en-us/news/uswnt-players-sue-us-soccer-for-gender-discrimination/l6cy1j1a65cm1uqaval9phk31.

[40] "Black Women and the Wage Gap," Black Women and the Wage Gap § (2021), https://www.nationalpartnership.org/our-work/resources/economic-justice/fair-pay/african-american-women-wage-gap.pdf.

Women have been earning more college degrees than men since the 1980s[41]. We are on track to make up the majority of the workforce. We are just as educated as men, with the same drive to enter the workforce and earn a decent living. Now, we are asking for more money. So why are we missing in top positions both nationally and globally?

If we truly want to see equal numbers of men and women in C-suite roles or elected as world leaders, we need to look beyond the actions of individual women who may or may not have asked for a raise or spoken out about sexual harassment. We need to dismantle and rebuild a system that gives only a select few women the opportunity to do so in the first place. At the rate that we are moving, we are still over one hundred years away from closing the pay gap at the global level. Why should we have to wait so long for equality and equity?

Movements like #MeToo, *Lean In*, and others have served a significant purpose, but the work is not over. No one can claim that they have solved the problem of systemic sexism in this country. Spending time with women, providing for women, or appreciating women should not shield a man from being accused of sexist behavior. *Being* a woman cannot excuse her from silently condoning sexist behavior, or allowing that sexist behavior to influence other men who might be watching.

Everyone is affected by systemic sexism. When we prevent women from reaching their full potential, we *all* lose. Now is the time to awaken. We are all players, and the time to speak up is now.

Awakening Action Item. Take out your journal and make a list of ten examples of when you believe you were the subject of systematic sexism, racism, or both. Give details of the situation: who was involved, how you felt, and how you

---

[41] Dani Matias, "New Report Says Women Will Soon Be Majority Of College-Educated U.S. Workers," U.S. Women With College Degrees Could Soon Be Majority Of College-Educated U.S. Workers (NPR, June 21, 2019), https://www.npr.org/2019/06/20/734408574/new-report-says-college-educated-women-will-soon-make-up-majority-of-u-s-labor-f.

or others handled the situation. Write down other ways that you could have approached the situation. Reflect on how you can move forward. Are there policies or conversations that could prevent these situations from happening in the future? Can you take the first step *today?*

CHAPTER 7

Mentors, Men, And Leaning Into Closed Doors

As the world navigates the complexities of gender inequity and the systems that hold it in place, many individual women are trying to navigate their own industry. Hard work alone will not be recognized by the system. Often, you need connecztions, clout, or a mentor to open up doors for you. Those "doors," including jobs, projects, or speaking opportunities, have been shut to women for decades. Just as they hold the power, men hold the keys. Women often find themselves searching for a male mentor who can (metaphorically) open doors for them. You can't open a door simply by "*leaning in*" to it.

While exploring the need for mentorship and the power that men continue to hold, we find the intersection between the lies and the frustrations of this system. Although men see the benefits of mentorship, they are not likely to offer these opportunities to women. For decades this was due to the lie that women were inferior, or that our value only came from our beauty or ability to care for the home. In the post-#MeToo era, men find themselves withholding mentorship opportunities for other reasons. They don't want to get "cancelled," "#MeToo-d," or they simply do not believe that gender inequity exists!

This creates a cycle of women *leaning in* to closed doors. Worse, it enforces the lies that we have been told about our inferiority to men and our "place" in the home or on the lower rungs of corporate America. The discrimination and denial of women in the workplace feels illegal; although it technically is, court cases show that the system (and its lies) prevail. In order to discuss solutions to problems of discrimination, we must think bigger than legislation. We must dismantle the system that has encouraged this discrimination from the start and create a world where we all work to lift each other up.

Is Mentorship Beneficial?

Systemic sexism is a system where women can show an effort, but men ultimately make decisions. Women can take their seat at the table, but very rarely own the table or make seating arrangements themselves. We often need someone to advocate on our behalf in order to begin contributing at work.

 This advocate is often a mentor. Yet, in *Lean In,* Sandberg found fault with the idea of looking for a mentor. She writes:

> I realized that searching for a mentor has become the professional equivalent of waiting for Prince Charming. We all grew up on the fairy tale "Sleeping Beauty," which instructs young women that if they just wait for their prince to arrive, they will be kissed and whisked away on a white horse to live happily ever after. Now young women are told that if they can just find the right mentor, they will be pushed up the ladder and whisked away to the corner office to live happily ever after. Once again, we are teaching women to be too dependent on others.

Sandberg's privilege is apparent, once again. People throughout history have gotten ahead because they know someone inside an organization who champions them. Men and women have both secured positions because of someone they know or someone who advocates for them. I have hired people, advocated for them, or given them a chance due to our personal connections. Even before I began searching for jobs, mentors guided me and helped me build skills that I would use for the rest of my career. Sandberg has written herself that men tend to get hired based on their potential, while women are hired based on their past achievements. The right mentor can help communicate and vouch for a woman's potential, helping them secure jobs "up the ladder."

Jeff Bezos, for example, created a leadership team for Amazon that contains one woman. Only four out of forty-eight of the executives at the top of Amazon are women. Is this going to change? Not any time soon. Bezos has shared that low turnover is the reason for the lack of diversity on his leadership team. He knows and relies on the (mostly white) men at the top. This reliability and familiarity is clearly important to his decisions.

An advocate or a mentor may be the key to securing the position that you want. Mentors will not dismantle systemic sexism alone, but they may be the key to rising in your industry as you awaken and shake things up. Why run away from that opportunity?

Sandberg has also found herself backpedaling on this issue. As the dust settled from the #MeToo movement, women saw a shift in how men work with women. Now, LeanIn.org has a page that shares statistics about the importance of mentorship and calls for men to mentor women, calling the process "critical to the success of women across industries[42]."

How Mentorship Shaped My Commencement Speech—and Career

I have personally benefited from the help of a mentor. In college, a mentor allowed me to pull myself out of a trap. Her guidance was the subject of my 2019 commencement speech at Charles R. Drew University of Medicine and Science. Without her confidence and investment in my success, I

[42] "Men, Commit to Mentoring Women," How men can support women at work | LeanIn.org (LeanIn.org), accessed June 7, 2021, https://leanin.org/mentor-her.

do not know if I would have completed my undergraduate degree.

Here's the story. I was a freshman adjusting to my first few weeks at the University of Chicago, and I immediately saw a disparity in the way that I spoke and the way that other students spoke (and were expected to speak, write, etc.). That difference was also noted by Angela, a well-spoken upperclassmen from Upstate New York. Angela told me that I had the worst diction she had ever heard and questioned my place at the university.

Her comments resurfaced every time I intended to speak. *Was* I fit to be a University of Chicago student? My fears and doubts prevented me from speaking in group settings for my entire first semester, so I enlisted her as a mentor and asked her to revise and edit my papers. Along the way, I studied grammar books and put in the effort to take on the King's English.

I have reflected on this mentor/mentee relationship in *The Huffington Post*, a commencement speech, and other keynote speeches. As much as I can credit my willingness to adapt, face my fears, and work on my grammar, I have to credit Angela. She was willing to put in the time and effort to mentor me. She could have easily shaken her head and let me sit in a stereotype that, more likely than not, would have held me back. But she believed I could improve, and her guidance allowed me to meet the potential that she saw in me. Networks, mentors, and advocates are critical to your development as a student, intern, professional, and leader.

I did not have a huge network of strong, professional women that I could rely on for advice in the early days of my career. I needed to create one. This is the type of work that women have to take on for themselves when men are refusing to serve as a mentor to women. Men rarely have to put in the effort to create a welcoming network like many women do. They often spend that time working on other ways to advance their career. By the time I started to create a network of professional women for advice, my male colleagues had already received opportunities, learned from mentors, and advanced their career further. This inequity is just the beginning of what holds women back as they try to navigate the corporate jungle gym, academia, or other fields that place value in mentorship and connections.

Leaning into Mike Pence's Door

Women are doing our part in seeking mentorship opportunities from men in our respective fields. But we are often met with the metaphorical closed door. Sometimes, this withholding of power or opportunity is subtle. Men simply do not reach out to women in their industries or make excuses for their inability to take the time mentoring female colleagues. Other times, this withholding is more blunt. When I think about men withholding opportunities from women, I immediately think of Mike Pence. Yes, *that* Mike Pence: the former vice president of the United States. One of his personal, rather than political, policies perfectly demonstrates why women cannot take on the brunt of the work to achieve equity or seek out male mentorship. Mike Pence refuses to eat dinner alone with a woman unless his wife is present.

Pence first shared this policy with *The Hill* in 2002, but his remarks spread like wildfire on social media after he secured the vice presidency[43]. The response was mixed. *The Washington Post's* Aaron Blake wrote an analysis titled, "Mike Pence doesn't dine alone with other women. And we're all shocked." Women criticized Pence's policy as a barrier to women staff who network, connect, and climb the ladder within Pence's administration. But not everyone felt that Pence's rule was bizarre or even sexist. Evangelical Christians

---

[43] Ashley Parker, "Karen Pence Is the Vice President's 'Prayer Warrior,' Gut Check and Shield," Karen Pence is the vice president's 'prayer warrior,' gut check and shield (WP Company, March 28, 2017), https://www.washingtonpost.com/politics/karen-pence-is-the-vice-presidents-prayer-warrior-gut-check-and-shield/2017/03/28/3d7a26ce-0a01-11e7-8884-96e6a6713f4b_story.html?utm_term=.34a9aeb43eea&itid=lk_inline_manual_2.

and Wall Street executives were not shocked by the news; in fact, this practice is more common than you might think.

At first glance, the "Mike Pence rule" does not appear to be a deterrent to women in the workplace. This rule does not explicitly try to prevent women from getting promotions, mentorships, or higher pay. Supporters of it may argue that it has nothing to do with business at all. Billy Graham and other Evangelical Christians (like Pence) adopted the rule as a way of avoiding temptation and infidelity. What does that say about the roles of men and women? Men can't be trusted to not sexually harass someone unless their wife is present? Women can't be trusted to not tempt men, even if the occasion is a platonic business meeting in a public setting or travel to a conference attended by thousands?

Any woman can see how this rule is ridiculous and fails to acknowledge how men and women coexist in the working world. When we take a closer look at policies and rules like this, we can also connect these customs to clear, yet indirect effects on men's and women's ability to work together in the workplace.

What happens when you do not *get* the chance to lean in? What happens when, out of a male's self-interest, he slams the door on you or any woman in the office? You can only lean into a closed door so much before you can't lean in anymore. If you are leaning into a man who is leaning away, gravity will get the best of you.

When I think about the *reasons* that men are avoiding business meetings with women, I can't help but get angry. Not all men use their religion as an excuse to "shut the door" on women in the workplace. In light of the #MeToo movement, some men are scared of getting "cancelled." Others simply overlook the women in their industry. Men may excuse their actions by claiming that women do not need any advocacy from men, that they are considered equals. But time and time again, the system reminds us through legislation, court cases, and everyday microaggressions that women are still not seen as "equals." We continue to be gaslit, ignored, and lied to. In order to stop these experiences from happening, we need male advocates and partners to join in the fight.

Men Are Scared of Getting "Cancelled"

How bad is the hesitation to work with women? Worse than you think. When the #MeToo movement started gaining traction, men didn't fight back. They retreated. Here are some of the findings that *Harvard Business Review* collected in 2019[44].

- Twenty-seven percent of men said that they try to avoid solo meetings with female co-workers.
- Twenty-one percent of men said they would be hesitant to hire women for a job that would require travel or other close interactions.
- Forty-four percent of men believed that other men will be more likely to exclude women from social interactions as a result of the #MeToo movement.
- Nineteen percent of men said they were reluctant to hire attractive women.

According to a survey sent out by LeanIn.org, 60 percent of male managers in the United States feel uncomfortable with mentoring, working alone with, or even socializing with a woman[45].

Yes, allegations of sexual harassment can briefly leave a stain on a man's career. But what men fail to understand is that they can avoid sexual harassment by simply not harassing women. Men have clear choices to make as it relates to their behavior. Mike Pence has the ability to have lunch alone with a woman in a professional manner without sexually harassing her. Male managers can have a solo meeting with a female coworker without displaying inappropriate behavior. Men do it all the time! If men are unaware of what constitutes sexual harassment, the answer is not to ignore half of the population. But they do.

---

[44] Tim Bower, "The #MeToo Backlash," *Harvard Business Review*, 2019, https://hbr.org/2019/09/the-metoo-backlash.

[45] LeanIn.Org and SurveyMonkey survey, February 22-March 1, 2019

When women talk about a "male privilege," we are talking about statistics like this. Men are not going to be turned away from mentorships, one-on-one business meetings, or golf trips because of their sex. These opportunities turn into jobs. Men may be given jobs because they know someone, because they're friends with someone, or because they're a relative of someone. They can rely on the opportunities to bond with men in high-powered positions in ways that many women can't.

If men refuse to mentor out of fear, where does that leave women who want to rise in their careers?

Overlooking Women in the Workplace

Men do not *have* to have a strict policy on excluding women to exclude women. Men do not have to be working in a position above a woman to shut the door in her face. Implicit bias and even careless mistakes will motivate men to exclude women, whether they are afraid of allegations or not. This exclusion happens *every day,* by men who have good intentions or who understand that being alone with a woman will not result in infidelity. The results are the same: when women are excluded or overlooked, they are limited in their opportunities to grow.

As the CEO of Butterflly Health, Inc., I know how frustrating it can be to be overlooked. I am the CEO of my company, yet I've experienced times where men have simply ignored me while mentoring other men. My brother is the COO of Butterflly. Together, we participated in weekly virtual meetings with a male mentor. I was excited to learn more about the health tech space from this mentor and build skills that would make me a better leader—until I found myself being overlooked. Every week for *several months*, the mentor made a habit to call my brother by his name (Rodney) without ever addressing me. He didn't acknowledge that I was on the call! All questions were directed toward my brother, even on topics where I was clearly the expert. If the mentor gave a compliment, it was also directed toward Rodney.

When I talked to my brother about this, he tried to defend the mentor. "He's a nice guy," he told me. He even tried to insinuate that I had been imagining the mentor's failure to acknowledge me. But my brother simply failed to see what I saw. The reason I brought the conversation to my brother was about the mentor's ability to be a "nice guy." He is a nice guy. I don't disagree with that. The mentor's failure to acknowledge me, the founder and CEO of the company, was not a nice move. He marginalized my position and elevated my brother's role in the company. I work very closely with my brother, but I'm still the CEO. And my brother was oblivious to how frustrating this was for me.

When I reflect on the incident, I was less upset with the supplier than I am with my brother (who has learned from the incident and has been forgiven). My brother was more offended that I called an individual out on their behavior, instead of being offended that I was overlooked as I conducted a business that I had founded, grown, and was running. Fortunately, this was a teachable moment and we have been able to resolve the conflict and move forward with a more critical eye of sexism within health tech startups. After we talked further, my brother agreed to pay closer attention to one of our calls. Afterward, he called me apologetically. Rodney counted how many times the mentor used his name and how he completely ignored me. He was convinced that I had been right and he too became incensed by the guy's sexist behavior. Women have to work to be heard, to be acknowledged, and to be seen. It's possible to get there, but we have to take longer routes and climb over taller hills than our male colleagues.

This may be one story about men overlooking women in the tech industry, but it's not the only one. In 2020, funding to female-led startups plummeted. The proportion of dollars to female founders fell from 2.8 percent to 2.3 percent. (Black and Latina women received just 0.64 percent of total venture capital investment between 2018 and 2019.) Few female-led startups become unicorns, or become valued at over $1 billion—only 10 of the 120 startups reaching this milestone in 2020 had a female founder. Meanwhile, only ninety-three Black women reached $1 million in investor backing for their businesses in 2020. This isn't because only 3 percent of founders seeking funding are women, or that .064 percent of founders seeking funding are Black and Latina women. Women are simply being overlooked, and this has serious monetary effects.

Men Do Not Think Sexism Exists

A lot of men think that because they see women in positions of power, or that they have female colleagues, that we live in a post-sexism world. They think that the #MeToo movement has led to equity. They see the less than 3 percent of funding that women get from VCs and pat those VCs on the back for giving women a chance. And why would men go out of their way to help women if they think that we don't need their "help"? Why would they mentor a woman if they think all doors are open to women, that a woman just needs to *lean in* or work hard to achieve success?

A 2016 poll asked men and women whether women still face significant obstacles in the workplace. Fifty-six percent of men said, "no[46]." In 2020, a similar poll asked men and women to reflect on the progress that women have made both in and out of the workplace. While 49 percent of men believe that more strides need to be made, 64 percent of women have the same feelings. Consistently, fewer men than women believe that sexual harassment, society's expectations for men and women, and a lack of women in leadership continue to be barriers for gender equity[47].

---

[46] Hannah Fingerhut, "In Both Parties, Men and Women Differ over Whether Women Still Face Obstacles to Progress," In both parties, men and women differ over whether women still face obstacles to progress (Pew Research Center, August 16, 2016), http://www.pewresearch.org/fact-tank/2016/08/16/in-both-parties-men-and-women-differ-over-whether-women-still-face-obstacles-to-progress/.

[47] Amanda Barroso, "Key Takeaways on Americans' Views on Gender Equality a Century after U.S. Women Gained the Right to Vote," How Americans view gender equality as 19th Amendment...

These numbers do not begin to cover the amount of men who believe that women's rights have "gone too far." These sexist ideas continue to blatantly look past a woman's talents or experience just because of her gender. Seventeen percent of men believe that men are better suited for political leadership positions[48]. One- in-ten men said men were better suited to management jobs than women.

These beliefs, as we know, fail to acknowledge the systemic barriers that continue to exist, the microaggressions that women face on a daily basis, and the doors that continue to be slammed in women's faces. Men do not have to face the same decisions about how to wear their hair or make the effort to avoid damaging stereotypes like women do. They don't understand that these differences between men and women are just a small part of a larger system that we are trying to break down and dismantle. That is why doors continue to close in our faces, we continue to be overlooked, and we have to work ten times harder to achieve the success that we envision for ourselves.

The "Mike Pence Rule" May Not Be Legal—but it Still Occurs

How do we fix this problem? To answer this question, we must acknowledge the attempts that women have made to illuminate the discrimination that women face every day in the workforce. Women have not just been denied mentorships because of their sex; women have been harassed, fired, and put in physical danger because their

---

(Pew Research Center, August 13, 2020), https://www.pewresearch. org/fact-tank/2020/08/13/key-takeaways-on-americans-views-on-gender-equality-a-century-after-u-s-women-gained-the-right-to-vote/.

[48] "Chapter 2: What Makes a Good Leader, and Does Gender Matter?" (Pew Research Center, January 14, 2015), https://www. pewresearch.org/social-trends/2015/01/14/chapter-2-what-makes-a-good-leader-and-does-gender-matter/.

employers believed the lies told by the system. Even though we live in a country with anti-discrimination laws, the lies prevail in a court of law.

Title VII of the Civil Rights Act of 1964 states that an employer, labor organization, training program, etc., cannot discriminate against an individual on the basis of sex (or race, color, religion, etc.). Legal scholars, including me, agree that makes the Mike Pence rule a form of sex discrimination. Yet, time and time again, the legal system allows this type of sex discrimination to take place. Instead of believing legal experts, judges who rule on these cases believe the lies. The following three examples will be extremely frustrating to read, but they are worth mentioning. They almost sound unbelievable, but rest assured – they are every bit real and damaging. We are *far* from living in a world where women can live without the fear of gender-based discrimination.

Denied the Chance to Follow a Campaign

Despite the standards put in place by Title VII, we still see examples of the "Mike Pence rule" barring women from spaces where they can work or advance their careers. In July 2019, Mississippi gubernatorial candidate Robert Foster denied journalist Larisson Campbell the opportunity to shadow his campaign[49]. He said that if Campbell wanted to accompany him, she would need to bring a male colleague. Foster cited the "Billy Graham rule" as a reason for the denial. Campbell was just trying to do her job. She had interviewed Foster many times and broke stories about his candidacy before. Despite her qualifications (and her promise to have her press badge showing at all times), she was denied an opportunity on the basis of her sex.

---

[49] Larrison Campbell, "Robert Foster, GOP Governor Candidate, Denies Woman Reporter Access Because of Her Gender," Robert Foster, GOP governor candidate, denies woman reporter access because of her gender (Nonprofit Mississippi News, July 9, 2019), https://mississippitoday.org/2019/07/09/robert-foster-gop-governor-candidate-denies-woman-reporter-access-because-of-her-gender/.

Fired For Her Clothing

If Larisson Campbell had taken legal action against Robert Foster, would she have won her case? The law says one thing, but recent history says another. In 2010, a dentist fired "the best dental hygienist he ever had" because the hygienist was considered a "threat" to the dentist's marriage. The hygienist took her former employer to court, arguing that he had violated Title VII of the Civil Rights Act[50]. Court documents show that the dentist had a history of telling the hygienist that her clothes were too tight, saying once that "if she saw his pants bulging, she would know her clothing was too revealing." The Supreme Court of Iowa didn't think that the dentist's comments were much of a problem. They overwhelmingly voted in favor of the dentist, claiming that he did not discriminate on the basis of sex.

Discriminated Because of Her Weight

Entire groups of women have taken to court because of a specific type of discrimination: weight discrimination. In 2017, I wrote an article for *TIME Magazine* on various court cases that allowed employers to discriminate against their female employees who gained weight. In 2010, two Hooters waitresses were told that if they didn't lose weight in thirty days, they would be "separated" from the company. In 2013, the Borgata Casino faced a lawsuit for prohibiting waitresses to gain more than 7 percent of their body weight throughout their employment. (Some were instructed to take laxatives as a way to keep their jobs.) Yet, these employers were allowed to continue these discrimination practices without legal ramifications, despite the health risks this poses for women across the country who are just trying to hold onto a job[51].

Legal analysts believe that many of these cases are cut-and-dry examples of discrimination. So if a woman were to

---

[50] Nelson v. Knight (Iowa Supreme Court July 12, 2013).

[51] Areva Martin, "Weight Discrimination Is Legal in 49 States," Weight Discrimination is Legal In 49 States | Time (Time, August 16, 2017), https://time.com/4883176/weight-discrimination-workplace-laws/.

argue that the "Mike Pence rule" is discrimination, would a court agree? If women who were overlooked by men or denied mentorship opportunities took their concerns to court, would they receive justice? I can't guarantee an answer. Federal legislation cannot prevent women from being fired, demoted, or barred from opportunities on the basis of sex. Our legal system, too, believes the lies that women have been told about our place in society.

The Mike Pence rule exists, weight discrimination is enforced, and women continue to be denied opportunities because our society places value on women based on their beauty rather than their ability to lead. Women are denied the ability to work closely with men who can advocate for them because we continue to be overlooked or not viewed in a professional light. Men who continue to ignore the pleas from women who want mentorship opportunities send a clear message: when they are in a room with you, they only see you for your ability to have children or take care of the home. They believe the lies.

Awaken and Rise

Women alone are not going to give women equal pay. We have been encouraged to proudly and boldly take our seat at the table, but what happens when that seat is "legally" removed because we do not fit certain beauty standards? What happens when the door is locked and we can't enter the room *with* the table? What does it say when women may take a seat at the table, but are not given the chance to *own* the table?

Individual men do not want to see *their* name next to the hashtag #MeToo. They believe that barring women from *their* office will solve all of their problems. Policies like this may protect individuals to some extent, but contribute to a much larger problem. The #MeToo movement gave women the chance to share their stories of sexual assault, but the movement was not enough to eradicate the problem entirely. It shone a light on the deeper motives of men, encouraged by the lies of the system. When men responded to the #MeToo movement by avoiding women altogether, they continued to set us back into times when women were expected to stay at home and men were exclusively given the opportunity to become the breadwinner. We have a lot more work to do.

Men have choices to make. Men in power have the responsibility to decide who climbs the ladder and who is excluded from the table in the first place. The *system* is built to separate men and women in this way. Men who overlook, ignore, or deny women are simply enforcing it. We all need to work together to dismantle the *entire* system and awaken to the possibilities of gender equity.

Awakening Action Item. Have you ever been blamed for failing to meet a deadline or not getting a promotion? Write down these examples in your journal and reflect on your feelings at the time of the incidents. Were other barriers preventing you from reaching these goals? How did it make you feel to bear the weight of the blame? When you were blamed, how did you react?

CHAPTER 8

Expectations, Norms, And Culture Are Holding Us Back

The system built the lies that are holding women back, but it is our expectations, societal norms, and culture that act as the pillars that support these lies. Implicit biases do not appear out of thin air. The stories we hear, the movies we watch, and the news that we read all form the idea of who women are, what we can do, and where we belong. Stereotypes of women, including stereotypes of women in color, are both established and enforced by the media we consume.

The journey from a story playing out in real life to a story being told throughout generations goes through many layers of filters and selection. The stories that we choose to tell and share go through a vetting process built by the system. And this vetting process affects what reaches the general population, from schoolchildren to TV watchers to the judges of the Academy Awards.

The lies told by the system tend to favor stories that enforce these lies. These stories set specific expectations for women: we are characterized as the subservient sex, one that does not ask for recognition or does not need to be seen as an equal to men. It's time to write, share, and award new stories. When our media and culture show women in a different light, when we are seen as breadwinners or equal to our male counterparts, we begin to see these stories being played out in real life. Life imitates art, and art imitates life. And our art can no longer continue to spread the lies of the system.

Representation Becomes Expectation

When someone hears the word, "stay-at-home..." they might automatically finish the sentence with "mom." The word "secretary" and the word "CEO" conjure up different images of women and men, respectively. Why is this true? All you have to do is search through our country's classic movies and TV shows.

Our expectations of men and women have been taught to us in school, in the media, and at home before we were born. All you have to do is look at a gender reveal party to see that our perception of a boy and a girl are different. Men are expected to be tough, strong, ambitious—playing in the dirt or with building blocks. Women are taught to be beautiful, demure, and to "know our place"—always looking dainty and only playing with dolls.

These expectations stick with us our entire lives, laying the path that we take on our journeys. The hero's journey, in movies and TV, often looks different for men and women. While a man goes on a journey to find wealth, glory, and power, women go on a journey to find love or family. Women, in the media, rarely go on a hero's journey at all. Instead, they simply support a man in his journey or wait for him to get home. Think about the action movie vs. the rom-com: who is the protagonist in these movies?

What Stories Are We Sharing?

Films and television shows simply do not tell stories with women and minorities in leadership roles. Shows like *Scandal, Veep,* or *Madam Secretary* may be the first time that viewers have seen women holding the highest political offices in the country, and these shows did not come out until the 21st century. If films don't equally represent men and women in roles as presidents, vice presidents, CEOs of companies, it's harder for women or girls to envision themselves in those roles. If all people see are images of white men as the CEO, as the COO, as the chairman of the board, as the board member, then that's what we will expect to see when we walk into a boardroom. We start to form the idea of what the world looks like, or even what it *should* look like. Men become CEOs because stories made us believe that men are *supposed* to be CEOs. Society places pressure on men and women to fulfill and perpetuate that narrative, upholding the natural workings of society and the ideals entrenched within.

But there is more to the idea that women haven't done enough to earn their role in the C-suite or in other leadership positions. We are caught in a cycle. Women have to work twice as hard to even get close to leadership positions because they are not given the opportunity to rise through the ranks and because women simply aren't seen as leaders. We aren't represented in boardrooms at work, and we aren't represented in the media we consume at home. When we fail to read or watch stories about women leaders, we do not expect women to be leaders. Combine that with the lie that leadership and accolades are solely "earned" through hard work, and we tell a pretty damning story of women who try to navigate the workplace and do not obtain leadership positions. Girls with dreams become women with influence. This is why we have to push for more representation in media, politics, and boardrooms!

Whose Stories Are We Spotlighting?

The answer, then, seems simple. We must tell more stories with women in leadership roles or highlight movies that portray an equitable society. There's just one problem: we fail to bring these stories into the spotlight.

The year 2020 began with a ninety-two-year-old tradition: announcing the nominations for the year's Academy Awards. Issa Rae, star of *Insecure,* read out the nominations for Best Director. Martin Scorsese, *The Irishman*. Todd Phillips, *Joker*. Sam Mendes, *1917*. Quentin Tarantino, *Once Upon a Time in Hollywood*. Bong Joon-Ho, *Parasite*. Once the nominations were read, Issa Rae said, "Congratulations to those men."

Some brushed the comment off as shade, but it spoke to the frustrations of women who saw themselves pushed out, once again, from the Best Director category. In the ninety-two years that the Academy Awards have given out Best Director awards, five women have been nominated. Only one has won. The frustration that Rae and many women felt at that moment was timely. Not only had women created phenomenal movies in the previous year (Greta Gerwig's *Little Women* and Céline Sciamma's *Portrait of a Lady on Fire* were two highly-acclaimed films), but recent campaigns like #TimesUp and #OscarsSoWhite had also drawn national criticism over the lack of diversity at the awards.

The historical snub of female directors not only speaks to the lack of recognition of women's work, but also sends a message about the stories that filmmakers view as "important." Look at the movies that the Best Director nominees directed. They tell men's stories. *The Irishman* tells a story about organized crime, with women only connected to the story as mothers or daughters. In *Joker,* Arthur Fleck interacts with six women throughout the entire movie. His skewed interpretations of their interactions frame each woman as just another person "out to get him[52]." The film *1917* contains a single female character. (On the bright side, co-writer Krysty Wilson-Cairns received a nomination for the movie's screenplay.)

The female lens in Hollywood is simply not brought into the spotlight, no matter how "hard" a woman works in the film industry. In 2017, glaring differences on movie sets revealed whose stories were considered "worthy" of winning awards. Of the top 250 films of 2017, 88 percent had male directors, 96 percent had no female cinematographers, and 83 percent had no female writers. As the 2020 Best Director nominations show, we haven't made much progress.

Movies are just one way in which society shares that message with people within our society. They set expectations and enforce norms that allow systemic sexism

---

[52] Beandrea July, "In Joker, Black Women Are Visible But They Are Not Seen," In Joker, Black Women Are Visible But They Are Not Seen | Time (Time, October 11, 2019), https://time.com/5696670/joker-movie-black-women-characters/.

to hold women back at home, at the office, and around the globe. If today's women want a guide or a roadmap, they can't turn to the most highly-acclaimed movies of the year.

We can cite studies and statistics all we want, but we know that these expectations and the lack of female-focused stories really make an impact when we live them ourselves. Expectations and stereotypes directly (or indirectly) cause small incidents like microaggressions, and larger incidents like the dismissal of the case against women who faced weight discrimination. Throughout *my* career, I have been doubted, undervalued, and rejected from positions because I did not meet the expectations that society had for me or for leaders. Women all around the country can relate.

These are the stories that are often whispered at women's networking events, but may not be deemed "important," like the stories told in the Oscar-nominated movies of 2020. But that is another facet of the system. We have believed the lies that women, and our stories, are inferior to men. Women in the media have been valued for our beauty before our accomplishments. All of the lies that I have described can be traced back to movies, commercials, or other types of media that "tell the story" of what it means to be a woman in America. In order to change the expectations that our society has for women, we have to change this story.

How These Stories Play Out in the Workplace

We cannot acknowledge the lack of representation of women in high-powered positions without addressing where women *do* appear in textbooks, stories, and the media. Instead of the Wall Street executive, women are the Disney princess. Instead of the war hero, women are the housewife. Instead of the CEO with the vision, women are the employees on the lowest rung of the company, carrying out orders without question. Instead of the superhero, women are the damsel in distress.

These roles and tropes do not stay on the big screen. We see colleagues, professors, and people in high-powered positions expecting women to play within these roles. If we "forget our lines," we pay the price in demotions, rejections, or the failure to be acknowledged for the person that we truly are. The expectations placed on women are no fairy tale.

These expectations come from the roles that women have been given from our patriarchal society. We are limited in our abilities to that of a subservient worker. If we branch outside of this role, our experience or talent is questioned. If our talents are recognized, we are expected to give them away for free. These stories not only share our experiences, but also reveal the lessons that we have learned and used to succeed (and help others succeed) later on in our careers.

Playing the Subservient Role

Kristin Jacobson knows firsthand how deviating from the stereotypical "subservient" woman can come with consequences. At the time, Jacobson was thirty, a recent Stanford MBA grad working as the director of marketing at a cardiac medical device company. Jacobson had been excelling at her job, but a new boss heard otherwise about her performance from the predominantly male sales force.

> She promptly demoted me based on their feedback and presumably was supported by the other male executives in the company. This was done even though I had been one of the most productive leaders and had created significant value for the company. I was told I was not friendly enough and not nice enough. I was running marketing for a 300-person company getting ready to launch a cardiac surgery product and that was the critical feedback. Needless to say, I mentally checked out of the company and started looking for other jobs. I literally did no work that moved forward the mission of the company for about six months. But I tried an experiment.

I was over-the-top sweet to the sales force. I complimented them, I answered the phone on the first ring. I mailed them brochures and slides and whatever else they asked. I treated every employee with sugar-sweetness. I acted as a glorified secretary rather than the executive that I was. To my great surprise and disillusionment, at the end of that period, I got rave reviews from the sales force. Even more surprising, I also got rave reviews from my boss and other leaders! No one seemed to notice or care that I literally got nothing else done. In fact, not long after that, I received a promotion and was given the opportunity to create a sales force for the disposable portion of the product, as well as be responsible for all aspects of onboarding all new hospital customers, including surgeon training, hospital reimbursement, and patient referrals.

That was when I learned the very cynical lesson that the corporate world expects women to be nice and funny rather than productive or useful.

Jacobson acknowledges that balance between likeability and getting the job done continues to be a tightrope walk for many women.

It is an incredible challenge for women to be likeable because being liked is often antithetical to what is needed to drive a hard bargain or make a good deal for your company or client. Being aggressive and assertive is necessary for success but not "becoming" of a woman, and certainly doesn't make you likeable. Defending your positions and taking credit for ideas that you put forth or achievements you made doesn't garner "nice points" when done by women.

This is the trap that many professional women find themselves in while working in male-dominated spaces. The traits required to lead or move a company forward do not always align with the traits that we see in the stereotypes that have been placed upon women in society. Falling back into these stereotypes, and playing the role of the "sugar-sweet," and subservient woman, doesn't allow us to make the strides that we need to later prove our worth when compared to men. The boundaries that women must set, balance we must walk, and expectations we must simultaneously meet and shatter are exhausting tasks on their own.

Pushed Out and Pushed Aside

Women are "allowed" the opportunity to work if that work is underpaid, underappreciated, and not threatening men's superiority in society. Nothing illustrates this better than the history of editors in movies.

During the time of silent movies, editing was a very manual process. Tasks included cutting and pasting, almost resembling arts and crafts. Women, including women without much experience or education in film, were given opportunities to edit.

Once editing was recognized as a more creative process, women began to be edged out of the editing room. Men were more frequently chosen over women to receive the opportunity to take on this more exciting and intellectual role. Although women were never entirely erased from the position, the placement and recognition of women editors continues to be underscored by the expectations that we place on women as a society. Today's big names behind Hollywood's biggest movies are directors, while female editors are left in the shadows. Quentin Tarantino, for example, is a household name. Sally Menke, a "truest collaborator" who edited Tarantino's films from 1992 to 2010, is not. Despite her ability to set the pace and tone of these highly-acclaimed films, her work (and name) are not as well recognized as her male counterpart[53]. When asked

---

[53] Jazz Tangcay, "Women's History Month: The Female Editors Setting the Rhythm, Pace of Film," Women's History Month: The Female Editors Setting the Rhythm, Pace of Film (Variety Media LLC, March 4, 2020), https://variety.com/2020/artisans/production/womens-history-month-female-editors-thelma-schoonmaker-1203521812/.

about the choice to hire Menke as the editor for *Reservoir Dogs,* Tarantino pointed out a woman's ability to "nurture" the films[54]. Even in these creative roles, women are reduced to age-old stereotypes and roles as the nurturer or caretaker.

Did you know a woman edited classic films like *Jaws* or *Lawrence of Arabia*? What about *The Irishman* or *Mad Max: Fury Road?* Not a lot of people do. While the award for Best Director is one of the top awards given out on Oscar night, the award for Best Editor is not as prominent. More fanfare is given to screenplays, short films, and supporting roles. When women *are* chosen to edit, they are chosen with the expectations to "nurture" or work in the shadows of male directors, producers, and cinematographers.

This journey reflects the lies that we have been told so frequently. Although women have put in hard work as the editors of blockbuster films, they fail to be recognized. Their work, especially in the early days of cinema, was reduced to the comparison of arts and crafts, rather than lauded for the creativity and vision it requires to edit a film. Once again, the woman's role in a project and our accomplishments are seen as inferior.

We Aren't Just Here to Help Out

In worst-case scenarios, we are shut out of the conversation entirely or our abilities come into question. In best-case scenarios, women are expected to use our hard-earned skills to satisfy the needs of other professionals without receiving fair pay in return. We are expected to be likeable, or "nice," a word that is too often confused with "pushover," or doing whatever we can to help, serve, and satisfy others. This devalues a woman's time, energy, and expertise in her field. It also fails to recognize the hard work that we put in in order to build our skills and resume. When leaders, organizations,

---

[54] Girish Shambu, "Hidden Histories: The Story of Women Film Editors," Hidden Histories: The Story of Women Film Editors | The Current (The Criterion Collection, September 12, 2019), https://www. criterion.com/current/posts/6582-hidden-histories-the-story-of-women-film-editors.

or other groups expect women to be subservient and ignore their value, they continue to perpetuate the lies of the system.

I have experienced this firsthand as a professional speaker. I live in California, but frequently received invitations to speak around the country before the COVID-19 pandemic. In two separate instances, I was asked to travel to Boston and San Diego to speak at a conference—for free. I would have to prepare two completely different speeches for two completely different audiences *and* travel to each destination. Traveling to San Diego was a minor inconvenience and would only require a few hours of my time, but speaking in Boston would require flying across the country. Neither engagement was paying an honorarium for me to give the speech. Through my network, I learned that this happens to women a lot. Men may receive similar offers, but are more likely to receive an offer with an honorarium up front.

The professionals in charge of booking had specific expectations of my goals by giving these speeches. I would have been giving the speeches at women-focused groups, with the goal of educating and empowering other women. Of course, this goal is a priority of mine, but the value of this work could not be ignored.

In both cases, I tried to negotiate. Could the company get a sponsor to pay my honorarium? Could they get a sponsor to pay for my extra day of travel and prepare to give this empowering speech? I knew they had the budget, but was told they did not have the budget for me; instead, both companies tried to make me feel guilty.

Earlier in my career, I might have heard the dismal offer and said "yes." I might have worried about ruining my relationship with the organization, despite their refusal to pay me for my time. I might have given away or devalued the hard work that I put into my expertise and skills. But I refuse to believe the lies. My hard work should be recognized *and valued.* I should not have to get paid less than a man for doing equal work. I am a leader in my field, even if I don't look like those who have been portrayed as a leader in our society.

Writing a New Story

These stories, and similar experiences that women face in the workplace every day, are a wake-up call.

After her "experiment," Jacobson turned to mentors and colleagues for advice. "While very disillusioning, there was an extremely valuable lesson to remember how important it is for women to be liked to get ahead. Thankfully, my female boss then taught me explicitly how to promote things I had accomplished in a way that got them noticed but also was not seen as bragging. These skills served me well in every aspect of my future career and were some of the most valuable lessons I learned."

My experience reminds me of the importance of knowing your value and knowing your worth, and being prepared to ask for it. This means being able to say "no" and to walk away when people, for whatever reason fail to see that value, too. Another company's budget has nothing to do with me, and I shouldn't have to bear the responsibility for someone else's poor planning or fundraising efforts. As a woman, we are undervalued due to the expectation and implicit bias that tells us we are less than men.

The movie industry as a whole is starting to acknowledge and understand how little they have valued women's work. Both *Wonder Woman* and *Black Panther* smashed through box-office records after they were released. These movies weren't just your average superhero story. They centered around a woman lead and a Black lead, two groups poorly represented in the superhero genre. Moviegoers were excited to see themselves finally represented on screen. But representation isn't just exciting, it's necessary for moving our society forward.

Women *are* heroes. Women are champions. Women are leaders. We can exceed the expectations set by a patriarchal and sexist society. Female leadership has not been fully represented in the media, our history lessons, or in the stories that we tell future generations. Yet, women still find ways to succeed and rise to the top. We shut out the lies. We write our own stories. As you've begun going through the

Awakening Action Items at the end of each chapter, you've started to reflect on your experiences navigating systemic sexism. How will your story end, and what expectations will it set for women who read it?

Awaking Action Item: Bring out the popcorn! Watch a movie that tells a different story about women in the workplace. Share this movie with your friends and colleagues.

CHAPTER 9

Rebuilding The System Benefits Everyone

Why do we continue to live within this system? Why do men, even men who believe that gender inequity exists, continue to uphold a system that has continuously lied about the role of women in society and what we are capable of? Why do some women, particularly women of color, back away slowly or even push *back* on the word "feminist?"

In order to move forward and rebuild the system, we must acknowledge the benefits that this process has for *everyone.* The feminist movement doesn't just benefit white women. Gender equity doesn't just benefit women. By rebuilding the system, we uplift all people, of all genders, races, sexual orientations, abilities, religions, ethnicities, and ages. The people who only want to advocate for one group of women are feeding into the lies about the status of our system and who it favors. The system doesn't just need tweaks, it needs an overhaul. In order to do that, we need everyone on board.

Who is a Feminist?

The words that we choose, and the images that we associate with specific words, can have a serious impact on the way that we approach issues of gender equity. Need an example? Let's take a quick look at the word "feminism." The damning stereotypes of a feminist, the whitewashing of the feminist movement, and the silence of men in the movement have prevented us from showing feminism for what it really is: a fight for gender equity.

Feminists Don't Hate Men

The word "feminism," and identifying as a "feminist," has been through a rollercoaster of bad raps and misunderstanding. Up until the last decade or so, the stereotype of a "feminist" portrayed in media and news stories was particularly unwelcoming to men *and* women. Feminists were depicted as angry intellectuals with short hair and tattered clothing. Holding feminist ideals and loving your husband or male friends seemed to be mutually exclusive. Often, the women in these images were white, leaving women of color to ask themselves what their role was in the overall feminist movement. The stereotypes and images of a feminist managed to keep many women *out* of the feminist movement, despite feminists' desires to lift women up and open more doors to women throughout society.

This is the system at play. For decades it has succeeded in separating women and convincing them that through hard work, beauty, and understanding their place, they too could live a happy life and build a happy home. In order to rebuild the system, we must rebuild the idea of who is fighting for gender equity.

I believe that feminism is about being strong. Feminism is about being independent. Feminism is about being unabashedly authentic. Most importantly, feminism is also intersectional, acknowledging the struggles of women of color, LGBTQ+ women, disabled women, and all other marginalized groups. Real feminists adjust each other's crowns and recognize that we are all queens.

By associating these traits, rather than one group of women, with feminism and feminists, I can easily see how a pop star like Beyoncé is a leading feminist in 2021 and beyond. She does not fit the image that has been fed to us of the angry, male-hating feminist. Beyoncé loves her husband. She loves being a mother. But she also has the ability, and wants all people to have the ability, to pursue her career and be a leader in music and philanthropy. Her independence and strength are part of her brand.

I see Cardi B as a feminist and a leader, too. Older schools of thought scolded women for sexually explicit behavior, arguing that they are putting themselves in a position to be objectified for the pleasure and benefit of men. Women like Cardi B and Beyoncé have pushed back on that association, arguing that their choice to write sexually explicit lyrics, strip, or be a pop star is simply their choice. This choice doesn't make Beyoncé, Cardi B, Megan Thee Stallion, or anyone who fights for gender equity less strong, independent, or authentic than a woman who wears more modest clothing or works as an accountant. Supporters of this idea do not see a difference between Cardi B and Gloria Steinem, as they are advocating for the same cause: a more equitable world.

Feminists Aren't Just White Women

Nowadays, the image of feminism has slightly changed. Instead of bra-burning intellectuals, the word "feminist" may conjure up an image of the 2017 Women's March. Women paraded through the street in pink hats, celebrating ovaries and "girl power." These images portray the modern-day feminist as a woman who may have positive intentions, but fails to consider the struggles facing all women, particularly women of color.

The reality of feminism is that the gains of the feminist movement come to women of color *decades* after they are already being enjoyed by white women. While white women won the right to vote in 1920, discrimination and literacy requirements acted to disenfranchise women of color from voting opportunities for the next four decades. It wasn't until the passage of the Voting Rights Act of 1965 that these racially-motivated practices were finally outlawed.

Feminist movements make claims that women make eighty-two cents per every man's dollar, the reality for women of color is much more dire. Time and time again, white feminists have alienated Black women. They have failed to recognize intersectionality, failed to highlight racial disparities, and valued white women's tears over Black lives. This conflict in activism not only highlights the tangle of racial and sex-based issues, but it also serves as a reminder of why many women refuse to identify as a "feminist" or support events like the Women's March.

Critiques of the Women's March and modern feminism look through more than just a racial lens. Some argue that womanhood should not be reduced to genitalia, as this perpetuates a narrative that transgender women are not "real" women. Others believe that wearing a pink hat is simply not helping the fight, especially when many women wearing those hats chose to vote for Donald Trump or belong to a political party that constantly works to repeal women's rights. An iconic picture from the 2017 Women's March shows three white women posing for selfies while a Black woman holds a sign: "Don't forget: White women voted for Trump."

I share this tension because we must acknowledge it to move forward together. Your view of feminism comes from your experiences and your choice of perspective. You can still call yourself a feminist while fighting against the lies that white feminists believe about the goals of modern-day feminism. When I think of a feminist, I set aside the pink hats and sole images of white women whose votes may not align with the goals of feminism. As a feminist, I recognize that I am both a woman and a Black woman. I recognize that the injustices I have experienced are intertwined. By reclaiming this label, I am making a statement as a woman, but I am more emphatically making a statement as a Black woman. That statement does not exclude any group of marginalized women. As a feminist, I fight for equity among all people— and *that* is what feminism is about.

Dismantling and replacing the image of a "feminist" requires intention, critical thinking, and an acknowledgement on the evolution of the feminist movement. Rebuilding the idea of a feminist requires listening to women of color and acknowledging that they have believed lies spread by the system. This takes time, but is a necessary step as we move to include all people in the fight for gender equity.

Feminists Aren't Just Women!

Small tweaks will not solve the problems that come from a system built to hold women back. Similarly, a small group of angry people calling for radical changes can easily become isolated by society. Only a large, intentional, and passionate population can break the foundations of our system and change the expectations we have for people in our society. If the entire population had had intentions of dismantling and rebuilding the system, it would have already been done by now.

We need everyone on board. We need men, women, and all people in all industries fighting for an equitable society. Our economy, education, and nation will benefit from gender equity—and we need everyone to believe this to be true. We can no longer let the lies tell their side of the story. People (men in particular) have long held onto the belief that "feminism" is "anti-male," and that feminist goals will result in the loss of jobs or power among men. This belief may also be tied to the idea that gender equity has already been achieved, and that setbacks are the natural result of women's lack of ambition or ability. Men may believe that women asking for *more* rights are just greedy or lazy. We can no longer ignore the lies that we have been told about women and our role in society. When I say we need everyone on board, I mean *everyone.* And we need everyone on the same page.

These conversations may be frustrating. Not everyone is willing to open their ears and welcome in new ideas, but everyone is *capable* of opening their ears and welcoming in new ideas. Men can gain so much if they play their part in dismantling the system and rebuilding our society. The first steps to making this happen are taken when they acknowledge the truth and stop believing the lies.

What Can Men Get from Awakening and Rising?

To reach men and people who still subscribe to the lies of the system, we need to make the case that diversity and gender equity will improve their bottom line and career opportunities. Men in particular can reap many benefits from gender equity, including:

- A reduced burden as the breadwinner of the family.
- Fewer fears caused by other men's behavior.
- Emotional freedom.
- An increased quality of life in a stronger country (and world).

Reduced Burden as Breadwinner

An equitable society, contrary to what people may believe, allows men to have more freedom. Pay equity among the sexes puts less pressure on men to bear the burden of being the breadwinner. Financial responsibilities no longer have to rest entirely on his shoulders. Living in a world where women have greater access to higher salaries gives male partners more opportunities to explore their passions, work part-time, or take on childcare responsibilities without the stigma of being a "weak" male. Men, like women, will have more choices about how they want to live their life or support their partner.

Fewer Fears Caused by Other Men's Behaviors

The #MeToo movement came with an unintended effect: men became fearful that *they* would be the next man to become a trending topic or a "cancelled" figure. Women cannot stop men from sexually harassing women; only men can do that. By dismantling a system that has allowed harassment and misconduct to happen without consequence, we can rebuild a system based on mutual respect. A society built on gender equity sets clear expectations and allows men to better empathize with women and understand what is or is not appropriate. Men will be more educated about what sexual misconduct looks like, and women will have more freedom to speak up when it occurs. The distinction between "jokes" and misconduct will not be so blurred. Men can breathe easier and work with women without fear.

Emotional Freedom

Shattering the expectations of what it means to be a woman or a man can also give men more *emotional freedom*. Men are not raised to express their emotions. Despite facing pressures to be successful, earn money for the family, and face all of life's other challenges, men are not encouraged to share the emotions that these pressures may cause. When men need help, they are not likely to ask for it. Women are more likely to seek mental health services than men[55], yet men in the United States are 3.5 times more likely to die by suicide than women[56]. We want to shatter the expectation that men have few emotions and a constant well of strength. Equity gives men more room to be emotionally vulnerable. This can save lives.

Stronger Country

An equitable society is not just a warm and fuzzy place to be. If men want to see a better life for their country and children, they should consider supporting true gender equity.

Gender inequity is a public health crisis in this country. When women cannot compete in the workplace, they cannot gain access to high-quality health care. Without access to high-quality health care for a woman and her family, the cycle of poverty continues. Without access to onsite daycare centers or policies that consider mothers and parents in the workplace, the cycle of poverty continues. With the expectation that women, including mothers, should earn less than men while taking on extra household and childcare duties, the cycle of poverty continues. The families stuck in this cycle are a reflection of this country's inability to recognize the worth of women, children, and all people living in poverty. This is not an issue of intellect, will, or laziness. This is about access and equity.

---

[55] Lea Winerman, "Helping Men to Help Themselves," *Monitor*, June 2005, p. 57, https://www.apa.org/monitor/jun05/helping.

[56] Centers for Disease Control and Prevention. Web-based Injury Statistics Query and Reporting System (WISQARS) [Online]. (2019).

Research shows that when women are kept out of the workforce, the entire country suffers. Gender parity can grow our country's Gross Domestic Product (GDP) by $4.3 trillion in less than five years[57]. Investing in women is investing in our country, and we *all* benefit.

We Need to Reach Men Who Feel Attacked

Men will benefit from building a more equitable society, but this argument does not always break through the fears and beliefs that men (and women) have about dismantling or rebuilding the system. Men have deep-rooted fears that lifting women up requires pushing men down. They worry that they will be passed over for a promotion that they have earned in the name of gender equity. They hold onto old beliefs about what it means to be a feminist or what the path to gender equity will "look like."

In exploring the path toward gender equity, we must explore the different ways that we can bring men along with us. This includes reaching them where they are on their journey, using empathy as a tool, and appealing to their bottom line. Everyone will benefit from gender equity: physically, emotionally, and financially. We need this truth to overpower the lies that men have been told since our society was formed.

Reaching Men Where They're At

People are much more willing to listen to others when they feel comfortable and heard. Conversations about gender (or racial) inequity are already uncomfortable. In order for men to understand your point, they will need to acknowledge

---

[57] "Growing Economies Through Gender Parity," Growing Economies Through Gender Parity (Council on Foreign Relations), accessed June 7, 2021, https://www.cfr.org/womens-participation-in-global-economy/.

that their reality is dramatically different than the reality of a woman. Unlearning is uncomfortable.

Creating a comfortable and safe space does not equate to coddling or hand-holding. The reality of inequity in America is frustrating and brings up emotions for *everyone*. The difference between men and women, however, is that women cannot run from frustrating incidents of sexual harassment or pay disparity. This is our reality, and the reality of our female colleagues, until we dismantle and rebuild the system.

We have spent so much time fighting against a system that is hell-bent on holding us back. Along with this fight comes anger, exhaustion, and frustration. Productive conversations about these issues, however, require us to put preconceived notions or expectations aside. We are trying to create a system with redefined expectations. The expectations we envision include those that men and women are equally invested in gender equity. Beginning a conversation with these redefined expectations creates a safer space for all.

Men may understand the emotional toll that their wives, daughters, and female colleagues bear every day, but they may not understand how we got here. Privilege, including male privilege and white privilege, allows people in power to go through their daily life without living the history of discrimination. Your colleagues may have positive intentions but fail to understand the context behind the calls for gender equity. Acknowledging this lack of knowledge allows you to meet men where they are at. At the beginning of your conversation, ask questions.

- What does he know about discrimination in the workplace?
- What microaggressions has he seen women in his office face?
- When he thinks of the terms "feminism," and "gender equity," what does he imagine?

These questions could also be used to meet white women where they are in regards to intersectional feminism. A white woman may not see the microaggressions or discrimination that their Black female colleagues face every day. The conversations you might have with colleagues, friends, or family could be baffling, but many privileged people have not awakened to the reality of being oppressed. Be patient and be kind. If a person's intentions are positive, you are moving in the right direction.

Reaching Men through Empathy

Not being heard and feeling undervalued are real fears for men; they are also a terrifying reality for women. One of the goals of the #MeToo movement was to show the exceedingly high numbers of women who have been victims of sexual harassment. Conversations, initiatives, and other exercises may be an approach to showing men the reality of working in an environment that is unwelcoming with goals that feel inaccessible due to one's gender.

I have experienced this as an advocate for neurodiversity. People do not always understand the reality of being a child or adult living with sensory issues. Simulations and role-reversals give neurotypical people a glimpse into the everyday struggles and inaccessibility that the autistic community has tried to communicate for years.

Similarly, a role-reversal headed by a company's HR team could walk male employees through the life of their colleagues, based on complaints or research on microaggressions in the workplace. If a man experiences being dismissed, ignored, or has to hear repeated explanations of topics that he is fully educated on, will he begin to understand why we are fighting for equity in the workplace? If he had to create a budget based on a female colleague's salary, would he understand why we are asking #PayHerMore?

Workshops and training sessions can take many different approaches to meeting men in the workplace where they are. I have attended and held many anti-sexual harassment trainings that do get through to men who could benefit from taking their advocacy one step further.

Men in anti-harassment training sessions have daughters, wives, mothers, and other women in their lives who would certainly benefit from a more equitable world. But those daughters, wives, and related women serve more of a purpose than proving a man's existing commitment to gender equity rather than a reason to fight for a more equitable society. The daughters of men sitting before me at anti-sexual harassment trainings have desires and ambitions. They receive financial support to go to college and graduate school. But these women may also be subject to harassment in the workplace. They may receive lower pay than their male colleagues. When they become mothers, they may feel pressure from their male partners to stay at home without the comfort of paid leave.

This is the central message of my talks at anti-harassment training sessions. The men before me are willing to invest their money for their daughters to go to college. Why are they not willing to invest in breaking down the structures that are holding their daughters back from success? Why are they not willing to change a culture that may victimize their daughter in graduate school, law school, medical school, or the workplace?

Men in these training sessions are proud of their daughters. They want to support their wives. When we have conversations with these men about gender equity, we must remind them that their daughters and wives are no different than the women we speak about in these training sessions.

Reaching Men (and Appealing to Their Bottom Line)

The same media that built the stereotypes of bra-burning feminists instilled these fears in men, the same way that media instilled the fear that the Black Lives Matter group was calling for Black supremacy. But the path to an equitable society doesn't have to line up with the demands that the media speculates from marginalized groups. When it comes to gender equity in the workplace, a successful path could be quite...normal.

The McKinsey Global Institute outlined six types of intervention that could help to bridge the gender gap in the workplace:

- financial incentives and support,
- technology and infrastructure,
- the creation of economic opportunity,
- capability building,
- advocacy and shaping attitudes, and
- laws, policies, and regulations[58].

These interventions do not require the sacrifice of jobs, pay, or titles. Shaping attitudes, for example, does not require anyone to give up their job or earn less money. Remember, rebuilding the system requires some creativity. Could "financial incentives" include incentives for companies to achieve pay equity? Can "capability building" opportunities reach women and men who are experiencing poverty? We do not have to coddle men or prioritize their comfort over our rights. We can achieve gender equity without causing physical or financial harm to men along the way.

We also do not need to get too creative to see examples of how a woman's success can also lift up men. A marketplace that encourages competition always welcomes room for more competitors. If a woman (or man) starts their own business, or achieves a certain level of growth within their own business, they create room for more seats at the table. A successful female CEO does not dampen the success of the men around her. According to McKinsey's *Delivering Through Diversity*, "Companies in the top-quartile for gender diversity on executive teams were 21% more likely to outperform on profitability and 27 % more likely to have superior value creation[59]." One could argue that putting a woman in the

---

[58] Anu Madgavkar et al., "How Advancing Women's Equality Can Add $12 Trillion to Global Growth" (McKinsey Global Institute, n.d.).

[59] Vivian Hunt et al., "Delivering through Diversity" (McKinsey & Company, January 2018), https://www.mckinsey.com/~/media/mckinsey/business%20functions/organization/our%20insights/

C-suite creates more opportunities for all people, including men, to improve their bottom line, rise through the ranks, and grow with the company.

A company that supports diversity, and follows through on this commitment, benefits everyone.

Not Everyone Will Want to Listen

Some men will be persuaded by statistics and sources like McKinsey. Others will awaken as they take time to empathize with their daughters, sisters, and colleagues. We all know a man who refuses to listen at all. Without intention to open his mind or challenge his current reality, a person will remain stuck in their ways and continue to believe the lies.

As we continue to dive deeper into strategies for reframing the fight for gender equity to *everyone,* I want to take a pause and remind you that educating others is not an overnight process. A history degree is a four-year process. We cannot expect every man to learn and fully grasp the nature of gender discrimination tomorrow. Awakening takes time. Awakening may require conversations with multiple men and women over many years. It is not your responsibility to hang back and catch every person up to speed, especially if that person is not putting in their fair share of the work.

Refer back to your values and your goals during this process. Not everyone will play the same role in the awakening. Some women are most helpful reaching out to the "every man" who is not quite up to speed. Other women are more helpful in pushing the women's movement further into the future. Do the work that speaks to your abilities and your values. Rise in *your* power.

Awakening Action Item. Write down at least five characteristics that you believe are used to define successful men vs. successful women. How does language differ when

delivering%20through%20diversity/delivering-through-diversity_full-report.ashx#:~:text=Ethnic%20and%20cultural%20diversity's%20correlation,likely%20to%20experience%20higher%20profits.

we imagine these two groups of people? How do these words play into the expectations we have for the men and women in our offices, at home, and in our circle of friends?

CHAPTER 10

Working Within The System Is Not Enough

Changing the system requires acknowledging big ideas, from the shortcomings of past feminist movements to the expectations for women set by the media. But these big ideas are just a piece of the system on which our society is built. Individual lies are supported and enforced by a big system that is interwoven into every facet of our lives. I am talking about a system that reaches our workplace, homes, health care centers, and all levels of government. This fight is far from over because it won't end with a single law, strategy, or solution.

The system doesn't just need tweaks. If we want to see gender equity in our lifetimes (or the lifetimes of our daughters or granddaughters), we need a full awakening. Gender equity benefits us all, and has the potential to support the fight for equity among all sexes, sexual orientations, religions, races, and abilities. But to build a society that benefits us all, we all have to do the work.

We are already starting to see grand strategies and reimaginations take place in this country. Drawing parallels between systemic racism and sexism gives us a peek into how strategies like "defunding the police" or "reimagining public safety" can be used to bring about racial equity. We must demand bigger, bolder structural changes to dismantle and rebuild what is currently holding many women back from success.

In order to create a world where women and men have equal access to opportunity, fair pay, and leadership roles, we must reimagine how we approach the notion of having (and holding onto) a career. We must reimagine the value that we place on men and women. We must reimagine the path to success, since hard work alone won't get you there. In some cases, we must look to other countries for solutions. In other cases, we have to get *really* creative. In all cases, we must be patient. Big, structural changes come out of small steps, but they take time. We cannot dismantle society and rebuild the system in a day. But we can *start* today.

Who Do We Look To? (The Answer Is Complicated)

In March 2021, New Zealand made headlines as it became one of the first countries to offer paid leave after a miscarriage. (India became the first in 1961.) The legislation did more than just secure Jacinda Ardern's position as one of the country's more progressive leaders, it illuminated just how far behind the United States is in terms of maternity benefits. This is just *one* small example of the progress that we need to make in terms of gender equity and one solution that can take us a step closer to a more equitable society.

For decades, the United States has been the only OECD country that does not offer paid maternity leave for *all* employees. On average, OECD countries offer *eighteen weeks* of paid maternity leave, often allowing mothers to earn at least 50 percent of their earnings as they care for their newborn. (Thirteen countries offer full compensation throughout maternity leave.) Additional policies in countries like Estonia, Hungary, or Sweden allow mothers to enjoy over a *year* of paid maternity leave[60]. Without federal guarantees of paid maternity leave in the United States, many working moms have found themselves facing choices between motherhood and career.

---

[60] "OECD Family Database" (Organisation for Economic Co-operation and Development, August 2019), https://www.oecd.org/els/soc/PF2_1_Parental_leave_systems.pdf.

In the United States, we have managed to close 72 percent of our gender gap, and not all recent years have seen forward progress. If we want to rise through the rankings (we are 53rd in gender equality, out of 153 countries), we must think outside our current system and reimagine what it means to be a woman (or person) in our country. But where do we look?

We already know small steps that we can take to be on par with other OECD countries. Take maternity leave. Iceland, the county with the most gender equality eleven years running, offers a minimum of three months of family leave for each individual parent, with an extra three months that can be split between parents however they choose. Affordable daycare is also more accessible to Icelandic families. Statistics show that three out of four Icelandic women work outside the home.

Offering maternity leave doesn't even put us on par with Iceland in *one* area of policy. Women have been fighting for decades to have a generous maternity leave policy in the United States, and yet, it's not enough. Maternity leave, without paternity leave, enforces the idea that childcare is a woman's responsibility.

Has this made Iceland a perfect and completely equal country? No. Despite their parental leave policies, it is rare for fathers to take a full six, or even three, months off. Women who do not take advantage of this policy are often shamed. A majority of housework still lies on the woman's shoulders. No country has achieved perfect gender parity, according to the World Economic Forum. Iceland has only closed 88 percent of its gender gap[61].

As we see with Iceland, putting a generous parental leave policy in place still fails to tackle the societal expectations placed on both men and women. Parental leave is not enough to lead us to gender equity; it can only be one step in a much larger strategy. Believing that a single policy change can bring about equity is believing the lie that the system just needs a few tweaks. We need broader solutions that

---

[61] http://www3.weforum.org/docs/WEF_GGGR_2020.pdf

give mothers and fathers equal chances *and* expectations to care for their child and home without the expectation of sacrificing their pay, job title, or opportunity to advance in their company. We need to dismantle the entire system.

Where Do We Go from Here? (We Get Creative)

Patricia Homan, an assistant professor and researcher at Florida State University, believes that dismantling systemic sexism requires that we recognize the connections between gender inequity and health. "The first thing we need to realize is that gender inequality in the United States is not only a human rights issue, but also a public health problem," she said. "Therefore, gender equity policy is health policy[62]."

Now we're getting somewhere, even if it feels like a niche solution. By recognizing that gender inequity is a national public health problem, we can see policies like parental leave or even onsite childcare facilities in a new light. They receive more weight when brought into legislation or before the head of a company. We can budget for them more appropriately. These policies aren't just building blocks or stand-alone policies. They are a piece in the puzzle of solving a public health crisis throughout this country. And all it requires is shifting our perspective and getting a little creative.

Homan also believes that addressing gender inequity begins with these small steps. "Policies aiming to close the gender wage gap, increase women's political representation, protect and expand access to reproductive health services, or otherwise promote gender equity also have the potential to improve health for all members of society." These are all

---

[62] Kara Irby, "Structural Sexism: FSU Researcher Offers New Perspective on Gender and Health Inequality," Structural Sexism: FSU researcher offers new perspective on gender and health inequality (Florida State University News, May 29, 2019), https://news.fsu.edu/news/education-society/2019/05/29/structural-sexism-fsu-researcher-offers-new-perspective-on-gender-and-health-inequality/.

building blocks that alone may not be considered "enough" to declare a victory in gender equity on their own, but they all have significant importance when it comes to health and improving women's ability to work. Reframing the fight for gender equity allows us to advocate for all of these building blocks together.

Again, this is just one perspective. Think of maternity leave or public health as the start of a larger brainstorm about gender inequity in society. Where else do we see gender inequity affect policy? What other lights can we shine on the lies we have been told? How can we "zoom out" and find ways to dismantle larger systems in order to rebuild?

Who Do We Need In the Fight? (Everyone!)

Single solutions will not rebuild the system. Small tweaks made by powerless people will not rebuild the system. Just as we need to welcome men to fight alongside us, we need to reach people who can implement big, bold, structural changes. And who are the people that currently allocate public health funding, set expectations for the workplace, or put people in power? Right now, the answer is Congress. But even then, we must look beyond their power and regard them as a piece in a much larger puzzle.

As of 2020, 127 of 535 members of Congress are women. If we do not have equal representation of men and women who are directly affected by and experience gender inequity, how can Congress properly discuss and vote on policies proposed to tackle gender inequity? Electing 127 women to Congress has been considered a win in the past, but we must think bigger. We must recognize equal representation in Congress, like the policies that they implement, as stepping-stones on a much longer journey.

Members of Congress can play a role in implementing the changes necessary to achieve gender equity, but the responsibility does not rely exclusively on their shoulders. The role of Congress is to represent the ideals of the people, and we the people elect them to their role. We must all do our part in implementing change and rebuilding society as a whole.

Change ranges from fighting for parental leave at your work, to speaking out against microaggressions, to setting different expectations and holding your partner, colleagues, or government officials accountable. Together, we create the expectations that tell women to cover housework while men hold the role as breadwinner. Together, we uphold these expectations. We perpetuate the lies and live within the system that created these lies. Now, we must reimagine the expectations and replace them with an expectation that men, women, and non-binary partners do their fair (or equal) share in earning income, childcare, and housework. We must tell, share, and gather excitement around the stories that depict what a leader, businessperson, or politician looks like. We must replace the lies with the truth about women and our place in society.

Federal and state elected officials do play an integral role in reimagining the role of people in society. But so do CEOs, women's rights and civil rights activists, historians, small business owners, and the employees who are directly affected by these changes. You have a role to play. I have a role to play. The tools in the awakening, including social media, access to lawmakers, and offering opportunities to marginalized groups, are accessible to all of us. If you can tweet, you can contribute. If you can connect and uplift women who have a dream, you can contribute. If you can contact a lawmaker or elect an official, you can contribute. Your age, race, or physical abilities may also factor into where you should focus your energy. What is important is that you recognize that the small steps you are taking are a part of a much larger mission: to dismantle and rebuild the system that is preventing us from reaching gender equity.

The solutions to gender inequity are vast, expansive, and may take time to fully replace the lies that we have been told. They require the help and effort of more than just leaders at the top. But don't forget: you are a key piece to reimagining society and creating a more equal space for future generations of women.

Bold Structural Changes Start with Small Steps

The fight against systemic sexism will never move in a linear fashion. Women have experienced great wins in the past one hundred years. We have gained the right to vote. Over eighty countries have or had elected a woman to serve as the head of state or government. At least 200 women have reached billionaire status. The 2020 Democratic Primary included at least six women candidates, including women of color. One of those women was elected vice president for the Democratic Party. But the wins that we have made do not trump the stagnancy and sexism that women have faced in recent years (pun intended.) Blatant sexism and racism are condoned in many jobs throughout the country, including that of congressman or president of the United States. We do not receive equal pay for equal work, despite legislation and nationwide movements calling to close the gap. If we want to see true gender equity, we need to acknowledge this stagnancy and do the work to overcome it. Will this happen with the election of a new president or implementing one policy? No. Does this mean we should condone and allow the stagnancy to continue? Absolutely not. The movement isn't over—we need to continue to fight from all angles, considering the perspectives of all women.

Gender inequity is interwoven into the economy, public health policy, and a culture that places specific expectations on men, women, and non-binary people in this country. In order to dismantle the systems that have held women back, we have to zoom out. We have to look at a much broader strategy that not only includes the implementation of certain policies, but also creates a culture of accountability that lasts as senior leaders come and go. Changes may take place now, but we must prevent them from becoming undone five, ten, or twenty years into the future. The new system that we rebuild must be as interconnected and strong as the one that we are going to dismantle.

Don't be mistaken: "small" steps, like advocating for pay equity in your workplace or calling out microaggressions, should not be neglected while looking at the bigger picture. Treat these policies as one piece in a much larger, more complicated puzzle. No puzzle can be completed without each individual piece, but the connection of two or three pieces is only the beginning of the journey.

Throughout the next and final section of this book, we will continue to look at strategies to change company culture, national culture, and an entire system based on holding women back. We are not going to be held back any longer. This is our awakening. You will identify solutions that may serve as your first steps toward changing the way that you live and work as a woman. You may also identify solutions that do not fit your current lifestyle or the goals you have for your career and family. All of this is okay. These steps are just the beginning, and choosing what works for you is worth celebrating. Your efforts, patience, and strength will not just serve as your awakening. On your journey, you will also begin to inspire others to change the world and abandon a system that has lied to us for so long.

Awakening Action Item. Systemic sexism impacts the clothes that we wear, how much we get paid at work, and the choices we make about our health, family, and lifestyle. Write down some of the decisions you made today that were impacted by systemic sexism. What decisions would you have made if sexism were not affecting your choices?

SECTION 3.

Solving The Problem

CHAPTER 11

Reimagine And Reflect

How do we begin to reimagine the role of women and their value in the workplace? The work starts with you. Look at the ways in which you can fight for yourself. Not every woman is going to take the same path, but every woman must begin by advocating for themselves. You must recognize your own value, set appropriate goals, and fight against policies that treat you as less than your male colleagues. Look at what you consider "success" for yourself and successful in the fight for gender equity. Understand that you have the ability to achieve that success, and you have the ability to lift up other women who are also seeking success.

This process will require facing imposter syndrome. You may find yourself having hard conversations with people who may expect to overstep your boundaries. Fighting for the success you deserve, in a system that does not expect you to obtain it, is going to be a struggle. This makes the process of assessing your value and identifying your goals even more important to our larger vision for the workplace, society, and the world at large.

The journey begins with five steps that are focused on the vision you create for your life, both in and out of the workplace. Let's begin.

Step One. Assess Your Value

Value propositions (props) and mission statements set the standards and expectations for a company. Clients know what to expect when they do business with a company that proudly displays this information on their website or marketing materials. Employees know what is expected from them and how their work contributes to the company's overall goals. Competitors see how they can differentiate themselves and fill gaps in the industry. What is your value proposition?

As you begin your journey, create (or reassess) any value props or mission statements that you have created for yourself. Take time to sit down, alone, and be honest about what you bring to a company, business, or to the world. Who are you? What talents or traits set you apart from the person next to you? How can you use your skills and experience to move forward?

These value props may come from your upbringing, experiences, or talents. I grew up in Missouri, surrounded by women who taught me the value of hard work. My work ethic and commitment to community both stem from my upbringing and early experiences. I bring these values to every job I have, from television appearances to advocacy work to building my law firm and starting multiple companies.

Your value props may be different. Maybe you are passionate about specific issues or are committed to a specific community not bound by location. You may be committed to rallying people to take action. Conversely, you may feel that your value lies in work outside of large groups.

Mission statements and value props allow you to make decisions about what is best for you and your career. You may find that your results at work speak louder than bringing an issue to HR. If this is consistent with your overall value and mission statement, that's okay. When you find yourself feeling guilty, lost, or unsure of how to move forward, refer back to your mission statement and value props. Let this build a strategy and help you choose tactics that will be most effective for you, your family, and your business.

Mission Statements Allow You to Set Boundaries

Value props allow you to set these boundaries consistently so your colleagues best understand what you will and will not accept at work. This may sound like a small piece of the puzzle, but it makes a big impact. Understanding your value props, and communicating them at work, does not just attempt to change company culture; it also allows you to set a boundary with colleagues. When you speak out, you are saying, "this is not an appropriate line to cross. Back off." But you may find yourself needing to set boundaries in other ways.

I see this happening in my business. Employees have come to my payroll manager asking them to change deductions. If the manager changes these deductions, the employee will enjoy more take-home pay. Most of these deduction changes are legitimate, but employees have used this as a doorway into less ethical requests. Once they know they can ask this of the payroll manager, they may try to ask for more. They may want a number to be fudged. Maybe they are applying for a loan and want their pay to appear slightly more or less than the actual number. In one experience, a payroll manager brought these concerns to me. What do they do?

Not only did I have to refer back to my value props and the value props of my company, but I also had to tell the manager to do the same. Some of these requests were not just unethical, they were illegal. The fact that an employee had gotten comfortable enough to make these requests of the payroll manager was extremely concerning. They were asking the payroll manager to risk their job and reputation for the sake of a few fudged numbers. My business prides itself on an ability to succeed without taking shortcuts or making exceptions to the rules. If employees were not living by these value props, then maybe they weren't a great fit for the company.

I told my payroll manager not only to assess their relationship with the employee, but also to set strict boundaries. They needed to have a serious conversation about what is and is not acceptable. I knew these conversations would be hard, but they would accomplish two things: setting professional boundaries with the employee and reaffirming the values of the company.

You are going to face moments like this at work. Colleagues may ask you to step outside of your comfort zone.

Boundaries, limits, and ethics will be tested. If you have a strong mission statement and understand your value props, you can more easily defend your choice *and* set boundaries that reaffirm your value as an employee and as a person. Like the payroll manager, strict boundaries will allow you to keep your job and reputation while maintaining professional relationships with your colleagues.

Step Two. Fight for Your Value

Value is not just an ability to speak your mind or commit to your community. Your value has more concrete measures. Understanding your value can help you fight back against microaggressions, closed doors, pay disparity, and other struggles that have been supported by the lies for way too long. Let's zoom into looking at pay disparity and see how this fight alone may be approached in different ways. When you assess your value props and understand your mission, you can better choose the method of fighting that works for you.

Fighting for the pay you deserve is a form of boundary setting. Start here. Once this has been achieved, we can start to dismantle the system by fighting for equal pay outside of your own company. Think about a state or federal, rather than local, level. Think about the expectations, norms, and culture that influence who gets higher pay. As we explore different ways to close the gender wage gap, you will see how our expectations of "men's work" and "women's work" directly translates into lower wages for women. Pay is not just dictated by a manager's decision or federal minimum wage.

As we fight for equal pay, we must remember the importance of shifting the expectation of where a woman belongs and what her responsibilities are at work. And this can be done in many different ways.

Indirect Ways to Fight for Equal Pay

If you have achieved a salary that you are satisfied with, look for other ways to fight for equal pay. Consider working with organizations who are currently on the frontlines to fight for legislation and standardized pay. Support these groups with your time, money, or by connecting them to people who can offer these resources.

Fighting for equal pay at your workplace may be less appropriate or effective than going to local, state, and federal officials. Both of these efforts can make a change that benefits you and other women who are fighting for the pay that they deserve. If we accept the gender wage gap today, we can't expect it to close tomorrow. So think federal *and* local. States and cities have the ability to set minimum wages higher than the current federal minimum wage. Reach out to local officials about supporting equal pay legislation. There is no reason that women are making eighty-two cents for every man's dollar (and the gap between minority women is even wider.)

Job Titles and Responsibilities May Be Dictated by Gender

Equal pay legislation vows to offer equal pay for equal work. But what *is* equal work? One way to change the expectations for your pay, or another person's pay, is to assess your job titles and responsibilities.

A title makes a significant difference in expected job responsibilities, and therefore, expected pay. Data show that job titles may vary between men and women performing the same job, allowing women to expect and accept lower pay for similar work. This separation of title, despite performing a similar job, prevents legislation from recognizing that unequal pay is being distributed for equal work. The path to closing the gender gap, in these cases, is changing the expectation of what person is appropriate for each position.

Here is an example of different titles causing pay disparities among men and women. Picture a "janitor." Now, picture a "maid." What sex is the janitor? What sex is the maid?

The United States Bureau of Labor Statistics places these two jobs in different categories. "Janitors and cleaners" are considered one job[63], while "maids and housekeepers" are considered another job[64]. Essentially, both of these positions are performing the same job: cleaning.

You will probably not be surprised to learn that janitors and housekeepers make different average wages. The mean annual wage for a janitor is $31,410, while the mean annual wage for a housekeeper is $26,810. That extra $4,600 each year could go toward building wealth, paying for childcare, or paying bills. There should not be a significant difference in these two titles that essentially have the same duties. One way to contribute to closing the gender pay gap is to look at the emphasis that you put on job titles, and how these job titles may play into the roles of men and women in society. At your company, are you hiring a janitor or a housekeeper? Share these statistics with the managers in charge of hiring and make them aware of how they can close the gender gap, too.

Asking for a raise, reaching out to lawmakers, and shattering expectations for men and women are all different ways to approach one problem: pay disparity. All of these solutions are valid. Which works best for you, your company, and the way that you can work to fight the lies?

Step Three. Accept and Assign Responsibilities for Job Advancement

Fighting for equal pay is one way to assert our value (and the value of other women) at work. We earn this pay through various job responsibilities, but are those responsibilities *also* reflecting our true value?

---

[63] "Occupational Employment and Wages, May 2020," Janitors and Cleaners, Except Maids and Housekeeping Cleaners (U.S. Bureau of Labor Statistics, March 31, 2021), https://www.bls.gov/oes/current/oes372011.htm.

[64] "Occupational Employment and Wages, May 2020," Maids and Housekeeping Cleaners (U.S. Bureau of Labor Statistics, March 31, 2021), https://www.bls.gov/oes/current/oes372012.htm.

We already know that women are more likely to be assigned busywork that holds us back, rather than tasks that use the skills and knowledge that we have developed in our field. Take time to assess how much time you are spending on "busywork," versus how much time you are spending on tasks that use your strengths and fall within your actual job responsibilities. Unless you are a caterer, you should not be the only person in the office assigned to leave your desk and grab lunch. Unless you are a secretary, you should not be the only person in the office assigned to take minutes or record calls.

The way that you set boundaries and adhere to your value props may include holding back when a manager asks for volunteers to complete certain tasks. Maybe you have an intentional dialogue about assignments that make you feel undervalued. Leaders and managers may not see how their "arbitrary" assignment of small tasks adds up to time away from your desk. Speaking up, loud and clear, will set expectations about the value of your time and how your time contributes to the overall company.

If you hold the role of "manager" or give out responsibilities to your team, be mindful of how you select people for different tasks or activities. Do not ask for volunteers. Equally assign office housework or other tasks throughout your team. Equal assignments ensure that the men on your team do their fair share, and one or two individuals are not always away from their desks because they constantly feel the pressure to take on extra responsibilities.

Step Four. Ask Yourself—What Does Success Look Like to You?

If you do not hold a manager or leadership role at your job, you may have picked up this book to learn the path to earning these positions. Managers, leaders, and executives reading this book likely want to push their success even further. But what makes a woman, man, or any person successful in their job? What does success look like to you, based on the value props and mission statement that you have already set for yourself?

When many people picture "success," they think of rewards, monetary or otherwise. Recognitions, bonuses, and shout-outs in the newsletter come to mind. These external motivators are important, but they should not be the only affirmations of your worth. If you do not have your own strategy for reaching goals and celebrating your achievements, you are missing out on an opportunity to celebrate yourself and understand your value.

Remember: Success Ebbs and Flows

I practice goal setting every year. These goals may be small, recurring goals, or goals that could take the entire twelve months to complete. Goal setting has allowed me not only to stay on track throughout the year, but also to take a good look at what I'm doing and shape what I view as success for myself and my career. This process isn't always perfect, but it always provides a lesson in the ebbs and flows of success.

For example, I had a really good year in 2018. I was co-hosting the syndicated daytime talk show *Face the Truth* on CBS, working as a legal analyst for CNN, and traveling the country to promote my national best-selling book, *Make it Rain,* at sold-out events. My nonprofit was growing and my firm was thriving; everything seemed to be fine. When I sat down to write out my yearly goals for 2019, I felt empowered. I set bigger career goals!

At first, I thought I was going to hit these goals. But the year had some surprises in store for me. *Face the Truth* was cancelled. A lot of projects fell through. When I looked at my goals at the end of the year, I realized that I hadn't reached *any* of them! Initially, I was devastated; but I had to go deeper. The goals that I had set weren't goals that could be accomplished in a year. The success I had achieved in 2018 was built on the work that I had done in the many years prior. I had to go back to the drawing board, reframe some of my goals, and keep working.

Be patient and supportive as you hold yourself accountable. Not all goals fit neatly into a one-month or one-year window. Allow yourself to roll loftier goals over into a two-year window. Earning a degree or breaking even on a new business, for example, may not be healthy one-year goals. I have found that being honest with my timeline gives me more room to focus on what I have accomplished over the year and celebrate my success. That works out well for me. Despite the pandemic, 2020 was a better year. I started working on this book. I produced and launched a new web-based talk show and podcast. Butterflly Health started to gain significant traction through major investments and partnerships.

Do you want to start your own business? Earn a position in the C-suite? Start holding leaders within your organization accountable for reaching diversity initiatives? These are goals that *you* have to define for yourself. No one else should be tasked with assessing your value, setting goals, and sharing your ambitions with the world. The awakening process begins when you see your ability to advocate for yourself and rebuild what the world looks like for women. It's not going to start and end overnight, which is why each step of this process is so important to supporting your journey and lifting yourself up through harder times.

Success ebbs and flows. Some years will be better than others; that's just life. Don't give up. Just keep grinding.

Step Five. Celebrate Others and Be Celebrated along the Way

Setting your own boundaries and defining what "success" looks like for you are solo projects. You must take responsibility for spearheading the effort to understand your value and make sure your colleagues see how you contribute to your company. But this is not just about your advancement at work. By leading the way, you create a path where women in future generations can walk toward their own success.

This is the larger goal: to create a space where women are expected to succeed, and acknowledged when they reach that success.

Rise above the Pressure from Other People

Most people struggle with this. We see other people succeeding and quietly envy them. Even when we have achieved success, we might feel tempted to put someone down. That's not what awakening is all about. Remember: real women adjust each other's crowns. They don't care how their crown looks compared to the woman next to them.

If you have read *Make It Rain*, you have probably heard a similar message. When I started working in media, folks constantly asked me when I was going to get my own show. These people often had good intentions, but the impact was the same. I felt like I wasn't doing enough, even though I had just started on my journey. If these folks had celebrated or appreciated the success I had, I wouldn't have felt so pressured or frustrated with my path. We have to be careful not to diminish our own success by looking at other people or letting others impose their views of what our career should be. I did eventually get my own show, but it was only when I was ready.

You have to learn how to resist this outside pressure and recognize when it moves from positive support to unhealthy expectations. You also have to remember that you may cross this fine line when talking to women in your circle. The women in your life, including your colleagues and friends, are on a different path than you. They may awaken in different ways. Their mission statement and value props look different than yours. Do not compare yourself to the woman next to you or feel like a failure when you see other women succeed. Be happy for your friends and colleagues who have made advances in their careers. Remember that you can be successful together. Setting your own goals and defining your value allows you to compete with yourself, not with others. Appreciate, celebrate, and lift up the women along this journey.

Build a Circle of People Who Will Celebrate You

Identifying your value is a strong shield against imposter syndrome. As you build these statements and define your value, assess how your team sees you. Ask yourself the following questions about the people who you work with, live with, and converse with on a daily basis:

- Do the people around you recognize your worth?
- Are they willing to say it out loud?
- Will they tell your boss, clients, or network that you bring value to your team?

If the answer is "yes," you have a good group surrounding you. If the answer is no, ask yourself *these* questions:

- Do these people tear you down before they lift you up?
- Are they jealous of the success you have already obtained?
- Do they have a habit of undermining your value, or staying quiet when you need an advocate?

If the answer to *these* questions is "yes," you need to take a serious look at who is around you. A lot of women spend time with people who believe the lies. They spend time with people who hold them back because they are jealous, toxic, or they do not want to see women advancing in the workplace. It's okay to have friends who are successful, but they need to be advocating for *your* success, too. If you are doing better than everyone around you, it's time to reach out to mentors or colleagues who are willing to lift you up.

On Your Way up, Don't Forget to Send the Ladder Back Down

Being celebrated and celebrating others is a two-way street. Remember, we are building a system where women are expected to succeed and properly acknowledged when they reach that success.

As noted in chapter four, Lorna Little is the CEO of St. Anne's Family Services in Los Angeles, and a national leader in early childhood development. She says that "one way to help people overcome their circumstances was by having someone in their lives who believed in them and helped them create a plan for a successful future." If that "someone" is a mentor, a colleague, or even a family friend, you may find yourself with more opportunities than a person without anyone to lend them a helping hand. Celebrating others and being celebrated is about finding a circle where you all believe in each other, create plans together, and applaud when those plans come to life. We can all help each other awaken and rise.

Attorney and author Corey Minor Smith feels the same way: "My dream vision for the future of female leadership is that young girls will imagine themselves in leadership and execute a plan of action to get there. The dream includes women making it a priority to be available as mentors, sponsors, and guides for young girls to see the possibility for their futures and help them on a shorter, less complicated path to get there."

A woman who knows what she brings to the table is not afraid to eat alone. Surround yourself with independent, determined women. Help each other out. Assess your value, define your success, and fight together. We are much more powerful together. Together, we can reflect on the world that raised us and reimagine one where our daughters and granddaughters do not have to hear the lies that we were told.

Awakening Role Model: Stacey Abrams

As a way to celebrate the women who are fighting to dismantle the system, I want to highlight an awakening role model at the end of each of the last five chapters. I'll start with Stacey Abrams.

In 2020, Stacey Abrams was on the short list for the vice presidency. Abrams is a Yale-educated lawyer who spent six years serving as the Minority Leader in the Georgia House of Representatives. She served for ten years as a state legislator. Her race against Governor Brian Kemp made national headlines as a harrowing example of how voter suppression can be used to keep women and minorities from winning spots that they may have earned.

When reports started circulating about Abrams as a potential vice president, Abrams began to speak openly about what she had to offer. She wanted to be Joe Biden's running mate. Abrams told reporters that she would make an excellent vice president, and that she had had ambitions as a student of one day becoming the president herself. Her openness quickly became subject to criticism. A Trump campaign spokeswoman called her "desperate," and told Abrams she was "embarrassing herself[65]." Analysts believed that she was too aggressive, too brazen, too willing to promote herself[66].

These assessments of Abrams came with pushback. What is wrong with a woman, who is campaigning for a job, telling people that she deserves the job? Abrams knew that her experience as a state legislator would be subject to criticism, and she used her voice to proactively defend herself from these critiques. When you remove any expectations or stigmas around being an "aggressive woman," all Abrams did was share her thoughts on why she

---

[65] Dan Merica and Donald Judd, "Why Stacey Abrams Is Making Her Case for VP -- Everywhere," Stacey Abrams is making her case for VP -- everywhere (Cable News Network, April 26, 2020), https://www.cnn.com/2020/04/26/politics/stacey-abrams-joe-biden-2020-election/index.html.

[66] Patricia Murphy, "Stacey Abrams Moment: She Shouldn't Be Biden's VP, but She's Changed the Game for Women," Stacey Abrams obstacle to Biden is inexperience, not self-promotion | USA Today (Gannett Satellite Information Network, May 18, 2020), https://www.usatoday.com/story/opinion/2020/05/18/stacey-abrams-obstacle-biden-vp-inexperience-not-self-promotion-column/5209615002/.

should be selected as the nominee for vice president. But the expectations of a potential elected official are so closely tied to the role of women in this country that many *failed* to see Abrams' ambition as anything but "unconventional." When a powerful woman touts her accomplishments and ambitions she is criticized, even though men are praised and admired when they talk openly about their accomplishments and ambitions. Ultimately, her ability to be candid about her ambitions may have cost her the role of vice president, but remember: success ebbs and flows.

Throughout the voting process, Abrams has been vocal and adamant about the unfairness of voter suppression and how it disproportionately affects minorities in this country. She led the way as Georgia registered over 800,000 new voters. Those 800,000 new voters helped turn the state of Georgia blue in the 2020 presidential election. When Joe Biden won the presidency, many people thanked Stacey Abrams[67].

This is why we have to reimagine the expectations for women in our culture. Criticism that we are "too ambitious," "too aggressive," or "too bossy" cannot hold us back anymore. Women have been expected to devalue themselves, to be thankful for a dismal paycheck, to accept the role as homemaker. Our awakening calls for a reimagination of what we can accept for ourselves, our colleagues, and future generations of women. Stacey Abrams didn't let her critics hold her back from her larger mission. She knew her value, fought for her success, and didn't hold people back in the way that she was held back. That is what makes her a role model for all women who want to awaken and rise.

---

[67] Austa Somvichian-Clausen, "How Stacey Abrams Helped Get out the Black Vote in Georgia," How Stacey Abrams helped get out the Black vote in Georgia | The Hill (Changing America , November 10, 2020), https://thehill.com/changing-america/respect/diversity-inclusion/525387-how-stacey-abrams-helped-get-out-the-black-vote.

Awakening Action Item. The five steps noted above can help you reflect on your career and where you are going in the future. Write the five steps down on a piece of paper or Post-it note and place them on your desk or somewhere you can see them daily.

CHAPTER 12

Address The Lies

Get excited about this new chapter in your life. Women have spent decades, even centuries, listening to the lies that we have been told and holding ourselves back. We have let the system hold us back. Maybe you have found yourself working, living, or networking with people who have held you down with the lies. But this is your story. Feel free to hit everybody with a plot twist.

Address the lies at work and home. You can start the awakening process for yourself and others by setting boundaries and speaking up.

Know That Many Women Are Starting over, Too

Our culture expects women to sacrifice their careers and hard-earned pay without fighting back. Our country has failed to acknowledge how the COVID-19 pandemic has disproportionately affected women, especially mothers. By acknowledging these lies, we can move forward and rebuild a system without them.

The COVID-19 pandemic hit the country like a ton of bricks. Tens of millions of people lost their jobs or businesses, entire industries have collapsed, and no parent is quite sure how long their child will be learning from home. COVID-19's impact was a one-two punch for women in the workplace. An overwhelming majority of child daycare industry jobs (94 percent) are women. By April 2020, women's unemployment rate reached 15.5 percent. Unemployment has decreased as states start to reopen, but women find themselves taking on extra work as they watch or homeschool their children. The unemployment rate hasn't fully recovered, especially when you take a look at the rates for Black, Latina, and other minority women. The rate of unemployment for women has not been this dismal since the 1980s[68].

We know the consequences of taking on childcare responsibilities over moving forward in your career. Returning to work may come with the pressure to take a lower salary. Research suggests that the pandemic may widen the gender wage gap by a full five percentage points[69]. Are we willing to allow this to happen? Should we allow the country to shrug its shoulders, accept the loss of jobs, and half-heartedly make up for the decades of progress that we have lost?

No! The COVID-19 pandemic is an example of why gender inequity requires more than a promotion here and a holiday bonus there. If we want to close the gender gap back to where it was before the pandemic, or progress any further, our culture must evolve. Expectations must shift. All of us must awaken and rise. You may be one of many women who feel like they are "starting over" in the post-COVID-19

[68] Olivia Rockeman, Reade Pickert, and Catarina Saraiva, "The First Female Recession Threatens to Wipe Out Decades of Progress for U.S. Women," U.S. Recovery: Women's Job Losses Will Hit Entire Economy - Bloomberg (Bloomberg, September 30, 2020), https://www.bloomberg.com/news/articles/2020-09-30/u-s-recovery-women-s-job-losses-will-hit-entire-economy?utm_campaign=news&utm_medium=bd&utm_source=applenews.

[69] Meera Jagannathan, "The COVID-19 Recession Will Widen the Gender Pay Gap - but There Might Be a Silver Lining," The COVID-19 recession will widen the gender pay gap - but there might be a silver lining (MarketWatch, August 12, 2020), https://www.marketwatch.com/story/the-covid-19-recession-will-widen-the-gender-pay-gap-but-there-might-be-a-silver-lining-to-this-she-cession-11597225748#:~:text=COVID%2D19's%20disproportionate%20economic%20toll,downturn%2C%20suggests%20a%20new%20study.&text=Women's%20employment%20rate%20also%20saw%20a%20greater%20decline%20than%20that%20of%20men.

world. Do not be afraid. This time you're not starting over from scratch. You're starting over from experience.

Use Your Experience to Set Boundaries in the Future

Most people have very few positive things to say about the COVID-19 pandemic. I will offer one: COVID-19 has forced many people to set boundaries and protect their feelings.

I do not doubt that you have had hard conversations with friends, family members, and colleagues because of this pandemic. Telling a best friend that they cannot see your newborn child is not easy. Scolding a parent for not adhering to guidelines is not easy. With inconsistent messages from local, state, and federal government, many people feel as though they must set their own rules and standards for self-isolation, quarantine, and event attendance.

Everyone seems to have their own opinion about what is safe, appropriate, and necessary during this pandemic. If you are not aggressive in setting boundaries, that opinion may become unsolicited advice, or the rules by which your relationship is run. Women should not have had to explain themselves for taking preventative measures against a pandemic that has killed hundreds of thousands of people in this country. Yet, many have. Although these conversations are hard, they give us experiences that we can use moving forward. Protecting your feelings and setting boundaries relies on your ability to identify the advice that is helpful and the "advice" that is shared for selfish reasons. If a friend, parent, or colleague only offers negative or undermining advice, you need to speak up.

COVID-19 has allowed many women to practice this skill at home or with friends. Even if you have had conversations or "put your foot down" on certain policies already, setting boundaries can still feel uncomfortable. Remember that these conversations did not just keep you and your family safe during the pandemic. Setting boundaries and having intentional conversations are the building blocks for changing the expectations of women in this country. Changing the culture starts with you.

Remember Your Values

A conversation about attending a wedding may not seem like the earth-shattering action that will dismantle and rebuild our culture, but it is the beginning. Choosing your safety over a friend's advice requires you to recognize and harness your power. Women have been long-taught to accept the decisions of others, ask no questions, and hold back from causing a scene. When you make a decision for yourself, you make the intentional choice to unlearn those lessons and replace them with behaviors that benefit your health, safety, and goals.

The sooner you can establish your position and have hard conversations, the sooner you can get back to your goals. Toxic people in and out of the workplace are distracting. They sap you of all energy. Negative advice will not move you closer to the one-month, one-year, or two-year goals that you have for yourself and your career.

Why do we wait so long to have these conversations? Why do we procrastinate or hope that the issues go away? Going against the lies makes us a vulnerable target. Fear of stepping out of these stereotypes isolates us. And after the COVID-19 pandemic, we all know how awful isolation can feel.

When you face these fears, consider your values. Do not allow yourself to be defined by the names and jabs that men have used to hold women back. Redefine your ability to set boundaries. Identify the strengths in your ability to speak up for yourself and hold others accountable. A reassessment of your values may also give you suggestions for approaching hard conversations or setting boundaries. If you pride yourself on your ability to innovate, for example, you may find it useful to brainstorm some alternative events or solutions to what your friends or colleagues may be suggesting.

We can use the ups and downs of the COVID-19 pandemic as a way to shift our perspective on protecting our feelings and having hard conversations. Many of our decisions in 2020 came with high costs: monetary, risk, or otherwise. But you accepted those costs as a way to protect your physical health (and the health of anyone at home.) This cost-benefit analysis must remain at the forefront of your mind as you continue to protect yourself, set boundaries, and move forward to your goal.

No success comes without a cost. You will face challenges at work and home. You will find yourself feeling disappointed. Friends may not agree with you or support every decision that you make. Colleagues may purposely work to undermine you. Bosses and managers will challenge you. When you face these moments, remember your values. You have the talent and expertise to overcome any challenge. What will your next move be?

Have Intentional Conversations

Practicing these conversations now will prepare you to have them at work. Communicating your expectations and standards allows you to be consistent. When someone fails to meet your expectations, you can more easily have a conversation about accountability. Your friend, colleague, or employee will already know what you expect and what you will accept. They will make decisions accordingly, and will have less to say when they are held accountable for those decisions. Articulating your expectations and holding everyone accountable may not make you the most likeable employee or manager, but it will earn you respect.

This is a long-term game. Through my work as an advocate, I have learned the value in playing the long game and accepting the ebbs and flows that come with this work. I think of this work like a sales career. Not every call that you make is going to be successful. Customers will slam down the phone and reject you. The best salespeople are able to shake themselves off and pick up the phone immediately after rejections, knowing that the next call may be unsuccessful, too.

The greatest activists and advocates of our time did not expect short-term results. They did not expect every battle to be won or every person to stay on board. The evolution of culture, the rebuilding of our system, and the journey toward success will never happen overnight. Allow yourself the patience to practice boundary setting and other ways to recognize your power. Awakening is not just about rising one morning and staying awake. It's about rising up every single day.

Do Not Forget These Practices at Home

Awakening does not just take place in the boardroom. If we want to change the expectations of men and women in this country, we must address the lies as they play out in the bedroom.

Motherhood comes with surprises. The rising demands of working mothers are often underestimated by new moms who are expected to balance a full-time career with full-time, unpaid work at home[70]. As COVID-19 required more children to learn from home, many mothers have taken on the jobs of tutor, babysitter, and teacher. We have all underestimated the toll that COVID-19 would take on our careers, work-life balance, and overall health. Mothers need to re-evaluate the role that they and their partner take in childcare, and all families need to re-evaluate how to navigate "the new normal."

Women cannot dismantle and rebuild a system on our own. We need to have conversations with our male partners (for those that have one) about equal responsibility at home and work. If sacrifices cannot be made, alternative solutions must be devised. Protect your feelings and protect your career.

---

[70] Claire Cain Miller, "The Costs of Motherhood Are Rising, and Catching Women Off Guard," The Costs of Motherhood Are Rising, and Catching Women Off Guard | The New York Times (The New York Times Company, August 17, 2018), https://www.nytimes.com/2018/08/17/upshot/motherhood-rising-costs-surprise.html.

Use the lessons of COVID-19 to set boundaries, have tough conversations, and set expectations about when and how you will work toward your goals in 2021 and beyond. This process may awaken friends, neighbors, colleagues, and government leaders along the way. Never underestimate your ability to change the world.

Not everyone will awaken immediately. Many will fight back against your efforts to shatter the expectations of society. Do not worry. The cost of angering a coworker or having a tough conversation is little compared to the benefits, rewards, and equity that we can win.

Awakening Role Model: Tera Stidum

We need to address the lies now to build a better future for ourselves, our daughters, and future generations. When we fail to address the lies, we run the risk of holding ourselves and other women back. Every woman has experienced a conversation, a policy, or just a moment in time when the lies threatened our career, our family, or our happiness in life. Using these experiences to awaken and rise is the solution. This is why I want to share the story of Tera Stidum.

Tera Stidum, a TV producer and business owner, was twelve weeks pregnant when she decided to tell her two female managers the news. One manager was single, just like Tera. The other was married with two children. Stidum told them she was expecting and was immediately embraced by her single manager. The married manager looked shocked. After sharing some brief congratulations, she said, "I thought your career was more important to you."

When Stidum shared this story with me, she told me how devastated she felt by the manager's reaction. This manager was a wife and a mother herself who had managed to become a boss in the industry. Stidum respected her, and was disappointed by the untoward reaction. Was her manager judging her for being a single mom at the time? Had she not accomplished enough? Was it a mistake to have a baby at this stage in her career?

Fortunately, Stidum's other manager called her into the office later that day. She looked Stidum in the eye and told her that she shouldn't let her married manager's comments bother her. She also said that she would be there for Stidum if she needed anything along the way.

Stidum continued to have positive relationships with both managers. She decided she wasn't going to let the first manager's words get her down, however much those words hurt. Instead, she used the experience as motivation to keep grinding. Today, she celebrates over two decades with a career as a successful TV producer. Her daughter is now eighteen, and will no doubt remember the experiences her mother taught her as she follows her own path to success.

If Stidum could go back in time, she told me that she would have spoken up for herself. Working in television, Stidum understands how important it is to address the lies. She says, "Two thousand twenty has been such a powerful year in having our voices heard, and I think that while we have the microphones, we need to keep on shouting, 'Not without my sister!' We cannot stop until everywhere we look, every room we walk into, has someone who looks like us, too!"

Awakening Action Item. Reflect on the goals you have for this year and the next. What boundaries can help you achieve those goals? Make a list of boundaries that you want to set, and schedule conversations to set and enforce those boundaries.

CHAPTER 13

Use Your Voice!

Speaking up against sexism is not always the easy and obvious choice. The lies run deep, and those who believe them will fight to defend them with all of their might. Women who decide to speak out against the system may face backlash for doing so. Change and accountability are always met with resistance, to some degree. But you have to use your voice: this is a solution that will move you closer to success and the world closer to a more equitable society.

Although some men have enlisted in the fight against this oppressive system, women must play a leading role in addressing the lies and using our voice to demand change. The work does not solely rely on us, but it begins with us. This is not an easy road to take. This is not a likeable road to take. Microaggressions against women who are shaking up the system range from focusing on a woman's physical appearance instead of her work, to calling her derogatory and offensive names. Women have made tremendous gains in the past decade, but we have not yet dismantled systemic sexism within our corporate culture or country as a whole.

This is the reality that you and I will continue to face as we address the lies and awaken. But we are not alone in this fight. We must remember the women who started this fight, and know that they (and we) are not the last to use our voice.

Call Out Microaggressions

Microaggressions are everywhere. They happen every day. We cannot tackle entire systems in a day, but we can call out microaggressions and how they contribute to systemic sexism.

Fortunately, women are not the only ones who have recognized microaggressions caused by misogyny. In 2018, a group of over one hundred business leaders got together to form the Male Champions of Change initiative. They published a report labeling six types of everyday sexism that take place in the workplace[71].

- Insults masquerading as jokes.
- Devaluing women's views or voice.
- Role stereotyping.
- Preoccupation with physical appearance.
- Assumptions that caring and careers don't mix.
- Unmerited gender labelling.

We can all remember a time when microaggressions threatened to hold us back. When a viewer attempted to scold me for dressing "immodestly" while I made remarks about sexual harassment, for example. They allowed their preoccupation with my physical appearance to drown out my message, one they clearly needed to hear. As a woman reading this book, I'm sure you have been reminded of insults, stereotypes, and assumptions that have kept you from moving forward in your career. Using our voice to call out these microaggressions can bring attention to their existence and how they support the lies that hold us back.

"This is Cultural"

The summer of 2020 was rife with political tension, to say the least. This tension became explicit when Ted Yoho, a Republican Representative from Florida, began to accost Representative Alexandria Ocasio-Cortez on the steps of the Capitol Building. *The Hill* reported that Yoho used words like "disgusting," and "out of your mind" to harass his colleague.

---

[71] "We Set the Tone | Eliminating Everyday Sexism" (Male Champions of Change), accessed June 7, 2021, https://championsofchangecoalition.org/wp-content/uploads/2018/04/We-Set-The-Tone_Eliminating-Everyday-Sexism.pdf.

The Hill also reported that, to no one in particular, Yoho swore under his breath: "f------ b----[72]." The exchange made headlines. Yoho gave a dismal apology for the "abrupt manner of the conversation," but continued to deny swearing at Ocasio-Cortez.

In response to Yoho's abysmal language, Rep. Ocasio-Cortez used her voice. In front of Congress, she reflected on the incident: "Representative Yoho called me, and I quote, 'a f---ing b----.' These were the words that Representative Yoho levied against a congresswoman. The congresswoman that not only represents New York's 14th Congressional District, but every congresswoman and every woman in this country. Because all of us have had to deal with this in some form, some way, some shape, at some point in our lives. I want to be clear that Representative Yoho's comments were not deeply hurtful or piercing to me, because I have worked a working-class job. I have waited tables in restaurants. I have ridden the subway. I have walked the streets in New York City, and this kind of language is not new. I have encountered words uttered by Mr. Yoho and men uttering the same words as Mr. Yoho while I was being harassed in restaurants. I have tossed men out of bars that have used language like Mr. Yoho's and I have encountered this type of harassment riding the subway in New York City. This is not new, and that is the problem. Mr. Yoho was not alone. He was walking shoulder to shoulder with Representative Roger Williams, and that's when we start to see that this issue is not about one incident. It is cultural. It is a culture of lack of impunity, of accepting of violence and violent language against women, and an entire structure of power that supports that[73]."

---

[72] Carter Sherman, "A Republican Congressman Reportedly Called AOC a 'Fucking Bitch'," A Republican Congressman Reportedly Called AOC a 'Fucking Bitch' (VICE, July 21, 2020), https://www.vice.com/en/article/bv8ydd/a-republican-congressman-reportedly-called-aoc-a-fucking-bitch.

[73] "Rep. Alexandria Ocasio-Cortez (AOC) House Floor Speech Transcript on Yoho Remarks July 23," *Rep. Alexandria Ocasio-Cortez (AOC) House Floor Speech Transcript on Yoho Remarks July 23* (blog) (Rev.com), accessed June 7, 2021, https://www.rev.com/blog/

The recording of her words has since been spread throughout social media. They were mixed with a Kendrick Lamar song as part of a TikTok trend showing women feeling empowered by and celebrating the representative[74]. By using her voice, Rep. Ocasio-Cortez didn't just stand up for herself; she empowered and gave a voice to women around the world who have experienced microaggressions and blatant harassment like this. This is the power of using our voice.

Assess the Time and Place

As women, microaggressions often put us in a specific dilemma: do we speak out or do we hold back? Even Rep. Ocasio-Cortez felt conflicted after Rep. Yoho's remarks. "So while I was not deeply hurt or offended by little comments that are made, when I was reflecting on this, I honestly thought that I was just going to pack it up and go home. It's just another day, right?"

In the end, the abysmal apology made by Rep. Yoho encouraged Rep. Ocasio-Cortez to speak out. There are times and places when it is more or less appropriate to use your voice and call out microaggressions and lies.

Earlier in the book, I described an incident with my brother and a mentor who had completely ignored me in meetings and undermined my value as the CEO of a tech startup. The incident was a learning experience for my brother. But did I call out the mentor on his sexist behavior? No. My brother and I decided that the potential costs of bringing up one incident outweighed the benefits that could be gained if the mentor decided to reflect on his behavior. Not all microaggressions need to be addressed, especially in an environment and relationship where your comments may

transcripts/rep-alexandria-ocasio-cortez-floor-speech-about-yoho-remarks-july-23.

[74] Kara Nesvig, "Gen Z Celebrated AOC's Birthday with TikTok Makeup Tutorials," AOC's Birthday: Gen Z Celebrated with TikTok Makeup Tutorials (Teen Vogue, October 14, 2020), https://www.teenvogue.com/story/aoc-birthday-gen-z-tiktok-makeup-tutorials.

not be well received. Having a conversation with my brother about the mentor's sexist behavior was more important and beneficial to me and our company in the long run.

Consider the Alternatives

As you assess your workplace, you may find that assertiveness is not accepted, even if it is encouraged in the office across the street. There is no easy answer to when you should speak out or when you might prefer to "pick your battles." Speaking out against a microaggression may be the "right" thing to do, but may not be prudent. If a battle against one offense costs you a job and puts you in a position where you must restart at the bottom of a corporate ladder, the battle may not have been worth the effort.

When you come across a situation like this, know that you do not have to let other people lie to you and hold you back. Thanks to social media and other developments in communication, there are alternative ways for women to use their voice without threatening their job. You may find that reaching out to an ally or partner is a more effective way to call out microaggressions or bring about change. Addressing the issue with HR may be more effective. Writing a social post, calling out specific people or remaining anonymous, may be the way to go. You have tools for calling out microaggressions.

Using your voice can also be as simple as walking away from situations that don't honor you. If you find yourself strangled by a toxic work environment, creating an entire business may be an alternative solution to constantly fighting with HR or taking it upon yourself to educate your entire company about systemic sexism.

As an entrepreneur, you have the ability to work for yourself and create an environment that supports women and encourages others to awaken. You choose the processes and policies that shape how your business is run. If you want to see equal representation between men and women, you can make that happen. Entrepreneurship gives you the opportunity to create a culture that prioritizes accountability, equity, and progressive values. As a leader, you set the standards that build a pathway for other women to awaken and rise throughout your industry. If clients, employees, or partners fail to meet those standards, you can pivot your business elsewhere.

Starting a business has allowed me to step out of the "model" for what it means to be successful. I built my own path to success. Entrepreneurship has allowed me the freedom and flexibility to make my own decisions about childcare and my schedule, too. The road to becoming a successful businesswoman isn't easy, but the benefits may outweigh the costs for you.

Using Your Voice Is a Risk That You May Have to Take

The simplest choices I have made as a Black woman on television, including my blouse or the way that I wear my hair, automatically put me in a position where people may not like me. But these choices are the way that I use my voice to address the lies. I will not allow myself to change the course of my career to be liked or meet expectations of people who may want to uphold the lies or support the current system. I aspire, through my advocacy and work, to shake up these systems, and replace them with something more equal for everyone. As you awaken and rise, you might also have to make choices and adjust your strategy based on your workplace and your team's understanding of systemic sexism.

Using your voice is a risk. Sometimes, that risk isn't worth the reward. But when it is, take it. This is work that has to be done in order to provide better opportunities for ourselves and future generations. Staying in place may feel safe, but it can ultimately undermine your value. You are capable of so much. When former First Lady Michelle Obama sat down with Tracee Ellis Ross at the United State of Women Summit in 2018, she acknowledged how the wins we've made can quickly turn into stagnation. "So many of us have gotten ourselves at the table but we're still too grateful to be at the table to really shake it up, and that's not a criticism, because for so many just getting to the table was so hard, right? You're just holding on."

This eloquently reflects the state of many women throughout the country. We have made tremendous wins. We have watched our colleagues and peers achieve high pay and leadership positions. But if we cling onto the table where we sit, we don't take the next steps toward owning or running the table. We don't recognize our worth. Our seat at the table was earned, fair and square. Women belong at the table. Once we have established that truth, it's time to take further steps. As Obama once said, "I think if we want our daughters to dream bigger than we did, then we have more work to do." You may have a seat at the table, but know that by using your voice and taking risks, you could buy the building.

There are many different strategies for addressing sexism, including social media campaigns or creating a network of women for support. But just like microaggressions are not the extent of sexism in the workplace, tolerating or fighting against these instances are not the extent of creating a more positive workplace. Misogynistic behaviors stem from larger misogynistic attitudes, which stem from a system that allows misogynistic beliefs, policies, and systems to exist and spread. The work does not stop at preventing microaggressions. Leaders like Rep. Ocasio-Cortez are fighting, day in and day out, for larger policies that will create a more equitable society. We all have our place in this fight together. And our place in this fight starts with small decisions.

Awakening Role Model: Cori Bush

When I think about taking risks and using your voice, I think of Representative Cori Bush. I had the opportunity in late 2020 to interview Rep. Bush on my digital talk show, "The Special Report." Her story of living on the streets of Ferguson,

Missouri, as a single mother and her journey to becoming a history-making congresswoman is riveting. Cori Bush has faced setback after setback throughout her career, but she used those moments of oppression and violence to empower her. After Michael Brown's shooting in 2014, she began to use her voice and fight back against police brutality. Bush joined protestors and spent 400 days in the street fighting for racial justice. During that time, she was assaulted. Police tear-gassed her. She was literally thrown into the air on the streets. This didn't stop her. The death of Michael Brown inspired her to keep pushing further.

Rep. Bush entered into politics only to be met by opponents determined to silence her and keep her out of office. In 2016, she was a candidate in the election to be a United States Senator representing Missouri. She lost the Democratic Primary. Two years later, she ran again, once more losing in the primary. She took risk after risk, knowing that she was a minority voice in a red state. But those risks are starting to pay off. Using her voice is moving her further on her journey. In 2020, she was on the ballot once again to be a United States congresswoman. This time she won, beating the incumbent Lacy Clay and becoming the first Black woman to ever represent Missouri in Congress. She is only the third woman to hold this position in her state.

Rep. Cori Bush is an example of a woman who is using her voice to reimagine public safety, public health, and public policy in the United States of America. Her passion for fighting for underserved populations shines through with every word that she speaks. She has faced immense setbacks on her journey. I can guarantee that she did not fight every microaggression against her, but she did not let them hold her back, either. I highlight her as an Awakening Role Model because for every loss or setback she faced, there was an opportunity for a win. So, think beyond minor incidents in the office. Think long term. You, too, can awaken and reimagine the barriers placed before you in your career, home, and country.

Loud voices are subject to criticism. Even the loudest voice won't please everybody. But do not be afraid to turn up the volume. Stay loud, and stay consistent. Call out the lies from behind a megaphone. Not everyone in your office is going to agree with you. Not everyone is going to see the world in the way that you see it. Not everyone is awake, but sharing your voice will certainly keep them from going back to sleep. Loud women get results, and loud women win! Use your voice, and use it out loud!

Awakening Action Item. Don't forget to celebrate your wins. The next time you speak out against sexism, reward yourself. Buy a nice coffee or sit with the knowledge that you are making a difference.

CHAPTER 14

Bring Men To Your Table

This book is just the beginning of a long journey towards awakening. In order to dismantle the system and combat the lies that we have been told, we must reframe how we individually look at gender in the workplace, in the home, and in society at large. Then, we must share what we have learned with others. Every single man, woman, and person has a responsibility to educate themselves and others about the causes and effects of gender inequity throughout our country.

Use your voice by holding discussions and holding space for all people. Your voice can encourage others to share, make mistakes, take action, awaken, and rise. Your voice can be a call with hundreds, thousands, or millions of responses. Let everyone hear your voice by giving everyone a seat at your table.

Not everyone is ready to awaken and rise, and not everyone understands the grip that biases can have on us throughout the awakening process. But you cannot leave anyone behind without trying to engage them in these discussions. A more equitable society benefits everyone. Even if someone is hesitant to unlearn biases today, they may be ready to awaken tomorrow or after more time has passed. These different ideas for events, discussions, and topics can give you different ways to reach people where they are.

Introduce (and Reintroduce) Men and Women Through Media

Representation is power, both in media and government. When we see women represented as powerful, strong, and "breaking the stereotypes," we give ourselves more fuel to move forward and defy these stereotypes ourselves. Consuming different storylines and watching different narratives play out can also be a lesson, a realization, or a catalyst for discussion among people of all ages. If you are not comfortable having a one-on-one conversation with friends or family, consider a movie night or watch party that makes room for discussion of gender inequity.

Be careful with the media that you select. Look for examples of movies and television that portray women outside of our "typical" roles of homemaker or damsel in distress. *Wonder Woman, Hidden Figures*, and *Scandal* all depict women in strong, smart, leading roles. Movies with female directors or screenwriters offer a fresh take on the roles that women aim to play in society. Looking for films, TV shorts, and books that fit the bill is easier than ever, but the search for media that properly represents women as independent protagonists shows how important it is to watch and discuss these narratives.

Do not just watch these movies and hope that they will indirectly make you or others less biased individuals. Dismantling comes before rebuilding. Have conversations with your partner, friends, and colleagues about these movies. Ask questions and encourage an honest discussion.

- Would the female protagonists be considered "outliers" in their field?
- Are the struggles of the main character relatable?
- If the movie told a similar story about your workplace, what setbacks or obstacles would you potentially encounter?

Movies and television can open up our eyes to different cultures and perspectives, but people may label these stories as "fiction" and move on with their day. Keep going deeper. Discussions about our real-life encounters with harmful stereotypes and biases make these stories more real and apparent as we continue to reflect on gender inequity in our everyday life.

Reflect on Stereotypes and Obstacles Together

Where else do we develop stereotypes about men and women? Movies and television are not the only places where we learn what to expect and how we "should" act. Our culture is tightly woven with these stereotypes and expectations, so the learning process is not always so obvious. When I discuss the effects of these stereotypes, I share stories like my godmother's suggestion that I become a typist. You may also recall lessons from your parents, grandparents, or relatives that directed you toward one stereotypical path or another. Maybe you learned by observing the division of labor at home, at a friend's home, and at school. Every person will have different memories that influenced their view on gender and what we can achieve.

This is the importance of discussion. Not everyone will recognize how these memories reinforced stereotypes or affected the person next to them. The lessons that your parents taught you and a sibling may be remembered quite differently based on your interpretation and other cultural factors. My godmother, for example, had good intentions when she encouraged me to be a typist. If we were to have a discussion about this comment today, she would not likely make the same recommendation to my daughter or other young female relatives.

Use critical questions to guide the conversation with friends, family, and even yourself.

- Where does one develop the idea that a man's place is at work, and a woman's place is in the home?

- How many times have you been turned away or discouraged because of your gender? How does that experience differ for someone of another gender?
- Why do we feel uncomfortable with the idea of a father quitting his job to care for his children, but not a mother?
- What kind of world could we live in if gender equity was achieved?
- What freedoms could men, women, and all people have if gender did not have such an impact on our job choices, treatment at work, and decisions about childcare?

These questions may be met with resistance, or even shame. We do not always want to recognize the biases and stereotypes that affect our decisions and judgements. But until we face this reality head on, we cannot dismantle them.

Do not be afraid to think outside the box while having these conversations. Dig deep. This curiosity and questioning may reveal answers and possibilities that never occurred to you before. The answers may begin to form a blueprint for making a more equitable world for you, your colleagues, and the next generation of children interested in your industry.

Have Resources Ready

Well-intentioned men will benefit from hearing your individual experiences, but you do not have to serve as colleague, historian, and training session leader. Your time is valuable. Unless you are holding a workshop and are being compensated fairly, you do not have to bear the burden of educating all of the men in your life about gender equity. If a man wants to educate himself, you can simply direct him to resources.

Books, podcasts, and documentaries on this subject have already been produced for these purposes. If a man wants to take time out of his day to become an advocate for gender equity, he will take that time.

Identify Your Partners

You should not exclude men from the table while having conversations. Women and men need to talk about these issues together: one-on-one, in groups, at work, around the barbecue, while changing diapers, you name it. Men may not "get it" at first, but these frustrations cannot lead to women keeping men out of the loop. If men don't get it, you have to keep talking to them.

In some circles, we call men who do the work with us "allies." But as we move forward, we might want to change this language.

An ally is someone standing outside of the movement. They cheer us on, hoping that we achieve equity. A partner isn't just on the sidelines; they are in the trenches. They take the risks that we take by calling out microaggressions or advocating for equity in society. Partners don't just understand the lies, they expose them. We don't want men to stop at allyship. We want them to understand that dismantling society elevates their well-being. We want men to be partners who see how their success is intricately tied with our success as women.

We can identify male partners only when we let them in. Privilege allows men, as well as white people and others with privilege, to ignore the struggles of marginalized groups. If men are excluded from the struggle of women in the workplace, they will remain ignorant. Men excluded from the conversation will not have the context behind our calls for equity. They will not know what they can do, even if they do have good intentions. Yes, this can be frustrating but you must continue the conversation and the pursuit towards equity.

No, we do not have to hold every man's hand through the education of women's rights. Men have avenues for educating themselves. But if we identify men who want to become partners, we can point them in the right direction and cheer *them* on through their journey, too.

Give Actionable Awakening Items to Men

Conversation alone can't help the men in your life see what women see every day. They may need time to process what their privilege has prevented them from seeing their entire life. Or they might want to rise up and join in the fight. Men who have taken the time to educate themselves already may be asking you, "What's next?"

How can we show men what moving beyond allyship looks like? We give them more homework.

The contributions of people in privileged positions are especially important when C-suites are still predominantly male. Male partners, unlike allies or those working against us, are not "holding onto" the table. They feel comfortable enough to shake it up and aren't threatened when a woman wants to buy the whole building. When men express a desire to awaken and rise, give them actionable items that will move their companies and industries toward equity.

Men should offer help *without* making assumptions. Men, first and foremost, must understand that their job is to *listen* to women. Instead of running a load of laundry and calling it a day, men should talk to female partners and ask what they can do to allocate household duties more appropriately. Instead of hiring a woman and calling it a day, men should run all hiring decisions by female employees and ask for approval. If men make decisions for their company without a woman's input, that decision is not guaranteed to help women succeed.

Remind men in your conversations that their resources and help should be allocated by women who are involved in their companies, social networks, and government.

Men must continue to check the biases that they and other men hold. The conversations you have with your male partner or male colleagues must continue. If and when a man refuses to listen, you may need to bring in men who have already moved beyond allyship.

Hold men accountable for checking their own biases, and then calling out biases that other men hold.

- When was the last time a male colleague called out another man for being sexist?
- What do they think when they hear about issues like the gender pay gap or harassment in the workplace?
- How do they personally approach childcare and household duties with their partner?

If a man can commit to dismantling their own biases and rebuilding a circle of friends that are respectful, critical, and progressive, they are on the path toward a successful awakening.

Men at the top must implement policies to enforce an equitable workforce. The decisions to offer parental leave, institute gender equity goals, and hold employees accountable ultimately come from people at the top. If those people are men, you have to find ways to reach them and advocate for these policies. Policy changes are just the beginning of the awakening at the workplace. But for men who do not know where to start, give them these ideas as actionable items.

Not able to reach C-suite executives? Men incapable of making these decisions at their company can still call for gender equity goals and start the conversation at the workplace. No matter where they fit in their company, they have a voice that is valuable and should be used to implement progressive policies.

Men must remember that this conversation doesn't just apply to the boardroom. As any working mother knows, gender inequity at home can have a severe impact on a woman's ability to be successful at work.

Talk to your male friends and colleagues about how they can be a better partner at home.

- Are your male colleagues having these discussions with their wives and girlfriends?
- Are they reflecting on how biases may impact what they expect when they walk through the door after a hard day at work?

- Can they take on more responsibilities at home, moving the household closer to a more equal environment?
- Will they plan to have open discussions with their children, friends, and family members about gender equity?
- What sacrifices are they willing to make for their children? What sacrifices are their female partner expected to make for her children? Are they equal?

If you are getting through to a male colleague, remind him to take actionable items in every space he inhabits. The way that he treats women at the bank, at the grocery store, and on the street are testaments to his ability to be a good partner.

Let Men Have a Seat at Your Table

Women have led the fight against the lies we have been told since the birth of our country. We will continue to do so, but we must also let men pull up a chair so we can lead them through tough conversations. A truly helpful partner will put his opinions aside and direct his resources appropriately, but he will not be able to do so unless he has direction from women at the head of the table. Men must be reminded that it is no longer *their* table.

Awakening Role Models: Marty and Ruth Bader Ginsburg

Mothers can't just set boundaries with their husbands. They need to have conversations with teachers, principals, and anyone else who may take part in looking after their child. A sweet story about the late Ruth Bader Ginsburg reminds me that using our voice can set boundaries and expectations when it comes to assigning parental responsibilities.

Ginsburg had two children while creating the ACLU Women's Rights Project, teaching at Columbia, and litigating national court cases. Her husband, Marty, was also working. Yet Ginsburg would be the one to receive calls about her son's conduct at school. Fed up with constant interruptions, Ginsburg told the school, "This child has two parents. Please alternate calls. It's his father's turn." The school called her husband. After that incident, Ginsburg told NPR, "The calls came barely once a semester and the reason was they had to think long and hard before asking a man to take time out of his workday to come to the school[75]."

This change started with Ruth Bader Ginsburg using her voice, but Marty was also crucial in enacting this change and giving his wife more room to focus on her career. He continued to commit to this equity throughout the entire course of their marriage.

Ruth Bader Ginsburg's husband cooked. He took care of their child when Ginsburg went back to law school. When he was diagnosed with cancer, Ruth completed assignments for him and looked after his health. When Ginsburg was being considered for a spot on the Supreme Court, Marty reached out to his network and made sure they understood how qualified she was for the position[76].

Not every couple or parent is Marty and Ruth Bader Ginsburg. Parenting in the age of COVID-19 has proven to be more challenging than any other time in recent history. I tell the story of Ruth Bader Ginsburg to remind you that awakening requires conversation and action from multiple

---

[75] Nina Totenberg, "Justice Ruth Bader Ginsburg Reflects On The #MeToo Movement: 'It's About Time'," Justice Ruth Bader Ginsburg Reflects On The #MeToo Movement: 'It's About Time' (NPR, January 22, 2018), https://www.npr.org/2018/01/22/579595727/justice-ginsburg-shares-her-own-metoo-story-and-says-it-s-about-time.

[76] Casey Cipriani, "What Happened To Marty Ginsburg? Ruth Bader Ginsburg's Husband Was Her Partner In Every Way," What Happened To Marty Ginsburg? Ruth Bader Ginsburg's Husband Was Her Partner In Every Way (Bustle, January 7, 2019), https://www.bustle.com/p/what-happened-to-marty-ginsburg-ruth-bader-ginsburgs-husband-was-her-partner-in-every-way-15533947.

sources, including your partner. Bring your partner to the table, and give them some work to do.

Awakening Action Item. What have you learned so far? Share it with your friends! Talk to a male friend or colleague about the takeaways from this book and what you envision for gender equity moving forward.

CHAPTER 15

Congratulate Women Who Are Winning

Women have done tremendous work and made outstanding gains in recent years. Before you put down this book and move forward on your journey, I want to remind you of those gains. Women all around us have been exposing the lies, working against the system, and helping to build a more equitable society for all. By acknowledging and celebrating these women, you can advocate for yourself. The most important thing that we can do to awaken is to uplift, mentor, and celebrate women. And that means celebrating you, too!

So let's take this final chapter to celebrate the gains that women have made in terms of education, workplace policies, and creating a new path for ourselves. As we reflect on these accomplishments, I will leave you with one final piece of advice: connect and uplift the women around you who want to win. Mentorship and networking are so important to dismantling the system and rebuilding a more equitable society. Surround yourself with independent, determined women. Then push each other to reach your dreams.

Take a Moment to Celebrate!

Despite the pressure of the lies we have been told and the expectations from a sexist society, women continue to push forward for achievements and policies that show our true worth.

Education

Women *have* been putting in the work. We have been exposing the lies. We have been making sacrifices when it comes to motherhood, our careers, and our free time. And that hard work has been paying off! Just take a look at the statistics when it comes to secondary education.

Women have been earning more college degrees than men since the 1980s. In 2005, women started to earn more doctoral degrees than men[77]. The National Center for Education Statistics projected that women would continue outpacing men, making up 61.3 percent of the population earning associate's degrees, 57.5 percent of the population earning bachelor's degrees, 58.4 percent of the population earning master's degrees, and 52.7 percent of the population earning doctoral degrees in 2020. Breaking down the data further, women throughout all races and socioeconomic statuses also outpace men in postsecondary education[78]. In 2019, women became the majority of the country's college-educated workforce[79].

[77] "Degrees Conferred by Postsecondary Institutions, by Level of Degree and Sex of Student: Selected Years, 1869-70 through 2027-28," Digest of Education Statistics (National Center for Education Statistics (NCES) Home Page, a part of the U.S. Department of Education), accessed June 7, 2021, https://nces.ed.gov/programs/digest/d17/tables/dt17_318.10.asp.

[78] Alana Semuels, "Poor Girls Are Leaving Their Brothers Behind," The Gender Gap in College Education - The Atlantic (Atlantic Media Company, November 27, 2017), https://www.theatlantic.com/business/archive/2017/11/gender-education-gap/546677/.

[79] Dani Matias, "New Report Says Women Will Soon Be Majority Of College-Educated U.S. Workers," U.S. Women With College Degrees Could Soon Be Majority Of College-Educated U.S. Workers (NPR, June 21, 2019), https://www.npr.org/2019/06/20/734408574/new-report-says-college-educated-women-will-soon-make-up-majority-of-u-s-labor-f.

Workplace Policies

University degrees have allowed women to get their foot in the door. We have physical proof that we are just as educated as our male counterparts. The journey to equity does not end there, however. As women navigate the workforce, we face additional barriers; but we have found wins in these arenas, too.

Our appalling federal policies on maternity leave have gained the attention of bipartisan leaders *and* companies within the private sector. Calls for paid family leave have come from both sides of the aisle. Changes have been made (albeit slowly). These wins offer us some hope. As individual states like California, New Jersey, and Rhode Island ramp up their paid family leave offerings, the nation may take notice.

Companies residing outside of these states have to make their own decisions about paid family leave and what protections are available to new parents. Fortunately, some of these companies have stepped up to the plate. Others have stepped up to the plate for mothers, but leave fathers with the expectation that childcare is for their spouses.

Any generous paid family leave is a win, even if it is simply on par with other OECD countries. Netflix, for example, offers one year of paid family leave for both mothers and fathers. Deloitte offers mothers an average of twenty-two weeks of paid leave, while fathers get an average of sixteen weeks. Snap offers women up to twenty weeks of paid maternity leave, and fathers up to eight weeks of paid paternity leave. These are wins for mothers who may otherwise have financial barriers that prevent them from being a mother and moving up in their careers and pay grade[80].

The wins that we have made do not just tackle financial or education barriers; they also take on barriers like imposter syndrome, harassment, or the system as a whole.

---

[80] Stacy Pollack, "6 Companies Redefining Parental Leave," 6 companies redefining parental leave (NBCUniversal News Group, March 20, 2019), https://www.nbcnews.com/know-your-value/feature/6-companies-redefining-parental-leave-ncna984946.

Creating a New Path

Entrepreneurship or starting your own organization are ways to step out of the system and create a new path with less red tape and fewer barriers. I have found success as an entrepreneur; so have many of the women I mentioned throughout this book. One story in particular comes to mind. I shared Camille Proctor's story in chapter 3: after her son's autism diagnosis, she had little choice but to walk away from her corporate job and spend more time at home. But that was not the end of Proctor's story.

One year after her son's diagnosis, she started The Color of Autism Foundation. The nonprofit foundation is dedicated to advocacy, awareness, and knowledge among Black parents, connecting families to local services, and providing one-to-one support. In addition to hosting parent training and support groups, The Color of Autism Foundation recently launched an online hub that supports atypical learners during the COVID-19 pandemic. As a part of the Autism Safety Coalition, The Color of Autism Foundation has helped to pass Kevin and Avonte's Law. This law, named in honor of two young boys with autism who wandered from their homes and perished in nearby bodies of water, gives schools and emergency responders the tools and training that they need to prevent accidental drownings, one of the leading causes of death among children with autism.

When I asked Proctor if she would do anything differently regarding her career and child, she said, "nothing." Proctor identified systemic issues that appear to hold her, and the mothers of other atypical learners, back. She was able to awaken and rise, and she vows to continue leading on a global level.

The system is designed to hold us back. By celebrating and building a network of women like Camille Proctor, Kristen Jacobson, Lorna Little, Mariah, and all of the women mentioned in this book, you can continue to fight for equity in your workplace and fight against the system that has been holding us back. Remember, it doesn't get easier; you get stronger.

Celebrate Women by
Mentoring Them

The best way to celebrate other women in the workforce is to offer your mentorship or connect women with mentors who can move them forward. My mentors have been a crucial part of bringing me and my company into spaces where we might normally be turned away.

After years of working in law and advocacy, I entered into an entirely new arena: health technology. This space is not one run by women, African-Americans, or other minorities. I could see the lack of diversity with my own eyes as I met with other entrepreneurs in the field and entered into an accelerator program.

My brother and I weren't accepted into the program because we walked in with a strong pitch and wowed the people reviewing our application. We had been connected with a mentor, a white male, through contacts in our network that liked the idea of our company. Our mentor's help proved once again that mentorship is crucial to opening doors that you might have otherwise found shut (with padlocks).

My mentor had previously been through the accelerator program. He connected us with the right people to hear our pitch and give us funding. He vouched for us, worked tirelessly with his contacts, and guided us through every step of the application process. On this journey, we were able to look at the history of the accelerator and the companies that they've supported. The accelerator had invested in very few Black companies. When I looked around the program, I saw very few people who looked like my brother and me.

Our company may not be so different from the other Black- and female-owned companies who applied for the program. Neither was our company a huge risk to take. But for many entrepreneurs, setbacks and obstacles begin to pop up when you're trying to contact the right people. Circles within health technology and similar industries are small. They're also predominantly white and male. Entrepreneurs with merit, talent, and worth had been turned away in droves, not because of their pitches, but because of their lack of connections. My brother and I were lucky enough to have an advocate that could help us break into the right circles. That advocacy gave us our chance.

Mentors, advocates, and support groups are often the solution for women who want to prove their worth and get ahead. No one should wait around passively to achieve *any* milestone in their career. Finding a mentor is a necessary, active process that begins with advocating for yourself. And just like dismantling the system, uplifting other women is the job of both men and women. Mentoring, being mentored, and creating a supportive group of women are essential to exposing the lies and writing a new story moving forward.

Awakening Role Models: Maya Humes, Nicole Tinson, and MacKenzie McClain Hill

If we want to see a change in future generations, we have to lift up women and people of color within those generations. Right now, I work closely with a few women who hope to grow their careers with the help of my expertise, connections, and network. Watching their progress is a reminder of the wins that we made, and continue to make, as professional women.

I shared Maya Humes' story in chapter 4. She is one of the young women that I mentor. Her father reached out to me because she was thinking of going to law school, but she was also very interested in politics and journalism. Having experience in all three fields as a fellow woman of color, I was the perfect person to give advice and help navigate the possibilities within her future career path.

After her father reached out to me, Maya and I had a conversation over the phone. We discussed law school, journalism, and how to get work in the media. During this conversation, she asked me if I would be her mentor. Of course, I said, "Yes!" Maya ended up not going to law school, so I helped her get an internship with a local paper in Los Angeles. Five years later, she has been able to get jobs and work as a staffer with multiple elected officials.

I don't think she had access to any other mentor with the political connections that I have. Although she is highly skilled and qualified for every role that she has, my relationships and connections have proven to be extremely valuable as she searched for work. Her series of wins began when she advocated for herself to her family, colleagues, and family friends. Maya is an excellent example of how mentorship, along with skill and passion, can put you on the right path.

Maya isn't my only mentee and family friend. I met Nicole Tinson through church; she was also considering law school. I helped her get a job at my nonprofit, Special Needs Network, Inc., and mentored her throughout her time at Yale University. Once she graduated, I assisted her through the process of moving to Atlanta and starting her own nonprofit. Our connection through the church was fortunate. As a woman of color, I know how difficult it can be to get access to women who are corporate CEOs or in other high-profile positions. Throughout my career, I had an extremely challenging time finding women in those positions who would act as a mentor to me. I take my mentees seriously and do not forget the power that my connections and advocacy can have.

Recently, I have started to help MacKenzie McClain Hill, who is looking to build her social media brand. She is an aspiring Olympic track and field athlete and lifestyle brand entrepreneur. Through our mentorship, I have helped her position her company on social media, prepare for media interviews, and connect with influencers who could boost her profile.

I highlight these young women because I can see the future in them. Women have come a long way since the founding of this country; women of color in particular have made tremendous strides. Do not forget this on your journey. Do not forget to congratulate women, give them strength, and invite them to have a seat at your table. Together, we are stronger. Together, we awaken and rise.

Awakening Action Item. Reach out to a woman who is working hard. Recognize her hard work. Find ways to uplift her and support her on their journey.

Conclusion

My work in health technology is directly aimed at everyday people who may be underserved and underrepresented as they seek mental health care. The right care can erase many barriers that prevent them from having or reaching the same goals as their neighbor. Health care, especially mental health care, can be the key to "leveling the playing field" and giving people the opportunity to awaken and rise in their own lives.

But health technology isn't the only area where I advocate for others. I have had the luxury and privilege throughout my career in law and media to speak with some of the nation's leading experts and thought leaders on racial justice, law, and education. They have seats at the table. They *own* their table. Their opinions and expertise help to form decisions that become national policy. As representatives for entire industries or populations, these experts craft messages that become the voice of the people.

I have also been fortunate in my career to serve as a voice for the voiceless. The "voiceless" are underserved and underrepresented, but they are everyday people. They struggle to pay rent and put food on the table. These are people that may not have a national platform, but have incredible contributions to conversations about race, the economy, health care, and the direction where our nation is heading.

In 2020, I started "The Special Report," a digital talk show that allows everyday people to have a conversation with leading experts and the nation's thought leaders. Every one of us has something important to say. Your personal experiences, like the personal experiences I share on my talk show and in interviews, are crucial to understanding the way that gender inequity supports and manifests itself in 2020.

Sharing everyday stories gives leaders an understanding of where we are and where we need to go.

Continue to Speak Up

I know that these conversations are not going to change the world in a day or two. My work as an advocate is no different than the work of advocates throughout history. Dismantling and rebuilding a system that supports gender equity is not going to happen quickly.

That's why I urge you to stay patient and check in with your mindset as you move forward. Do not allow yourself to get burned out by this work. Create goals, but stay realistic. Set milestones along the way so you can check in with your progress every month, quarter, or year. Give yourself room to stumble, rest, and change direction. The goals and solutions that I have shared in this book go beyond a month's or a year's work. Do not fool yourself into thinking that your work will be done within one month or two. Gender equity will not be a reality in 2021, the 2020s, or even our lifetimes. If you are dedicated to advocating and fighting for gender equity, expect your involvement to last for decades.

You will get frustrated. I get frustrated. When I feel impatient, I remember iconic civil rights leaders like John Lewis, C.T. Vivian, and Marsha P. Johnson. They dedicated their entire lives to equity and justice for all. These leaders were not able to see true equity realized in their lifetimes, but their work became a catalyst for movements that have lasted for generations. Do I think one moment, hashtag, or policy is going to dismantle and rebuild the systems that hold women and minorities back? No. But this moment, this movement, and you as an individual can be a catalyst, too. As you move from this moment and continue fighting, you can't give up. You cannot let slow movement deter you from fighting. Take breaks, rest, and set aside time for self-care, but never give up.

This book is the result of decades upon decades of fighting by generations of women before us. Multiple "waves" of feminism have called for different paths toward gender equality and equity. The right to vote, the right to vote for *all* women, greater access to health care, and a general awareness of systemic sexism were all goals at some point in the feminist movement.

In 2021 and beyond, we are asking for more. General awareness of the issues falls short of the larger goals. We want to see equal representation in C-suites and political offices, not just a small percentage of women chosen to meet dismal diversity standards. We want to close the gender pay gap and never look back. Expectations should not hold us back anymore; we want to see a world where women and men receive equal opportunities because we believe without a doubt that women are capable of achieving just as much as men.

Our goals are lofty, but not impossible. Envisioning a world that makes room for equity may require a little "reimagination." This is one of the many parallels that we will continue to observe between the fight for gender equity *and* the fight for racial equity in the United States. But think of how far we have come in the movement for equal rights. The steps that we take today will be in the history books tomorrow. What do you want your children and grandchildren to read when they learn about today's intersectional feminist movement?

A Long Way to Awakening

History books today tell the tales of brave women fighting for the right to vote (although the details about *which* women initially gained the right to vote are often left out). Women have certainly made a lot of progress in the past century. We can now cast our vote to put women in office who will continue to fight for pay equity, national parental leave policies, and equal rights for all. Every single state has elected a woman to either the United States House of Representatives or the United States Senate. Representation is rising in government, as well as in corporate America and popular media. Stories of female political figures, sports stars, and leaders offer inspiration to the next generation of girls.

We must use these achievements not as an excuse to slow down, but as motivation to continue rising. Our success does not diminish the setbacks that women still face at work, home, and out in society. Stereotypes and expectations continue to support barriers that hold women back. Requests for equal pay are denied. If equal pay is achieved, retroactive pay or other required resources are not considered. The systems that keep our society moving are still engrained with sexism, racism, and other forms of bigotry that aim to reduce the worth and role of women.

If we want to achieve gender equity, we must dismantle and rebuild the system. History books in future generations will acknowledge the work, persistence, and cooperation that went into this fight and ultimately allowed us to awaken and rise. They will highlight the people that used their voices to destroy the foundations of a society that did not have their best interests in mind. You have a strong voice, one that deserves to be heard and recorded for generations of women. Use your voice. Awaken, and rise.

Acknowledgements

Reflecting back on the writing of this book, I owe a debt of gratitude to the women, mothers, and frontline workers who did so much during the COVID-19 pandemic to support their children and families and whose fortitude and focus inspired me every day over the past fifteen months. Too often, these women remain in the shadows toiling and sacrificing for their families and communities. Many work multiple minimum wage jobs just to put food on the table and to secure housing and transportation for their loved ones. They are the foundations and bearing walls of our fragile society. Their strength and sacrifice, like the sacrifice of the many women that I grew up with in the St. Louis housing project that I called home, encourage and inspire me to work harder and do more—and recommit to building a better future for women like them.

I also want to thank Black women from Harriet Tubman to Rosa Parks who have been on the forefront fighting for equality and the rights of all people and whose contributions to the effort for women's rights are often overlooked. I know that I stand on the shoulders of incredible women who dedicated their lives to winning the freedoms that we enjoy today. My journey from a housing project to the world's top academic institution would not have been possible but for the steadfast vision and perseverance of these pioneers. They dreamed of a better life for future generations and they sacrificed everything for the dream to become reality for millions of African-American girls and women. I also write in gratitude to the new generation of voices and activists, like the writer Chimamanda Ngozi Adichie, whose words reignited a global conversation about feminism and equity for all.

I also must acknowledge Sandra Bland and Breonna Taylor and the many women like them whose young lives and futures were stolen from them. Their deaths inspired whole movements that have forced an unflinching look at the unjust systems that keep us from being free; in their memory, we continue the fight for justice and true liberation.

I would be remiss if I didn't acknowledge my family and extended family who have played such a critical role in shaping me into the woman, mother, and advocate I am today. Thank you to my loving family–Ernest, Michael, Morgan, and Marty–there are no words for my deep gratitude for your sacrifices and support. You are the wind beneath my wings.

Although they have passed on, every year my love and respect for my mother Doris, my grandmother Doveanne, and my godmother Ethel grow exponentially. Every time I share my stories of growing up in St. Louis in the Carr Square Village, I am reminded of the giant shoulders I stand on and the profound impact each of you had on my life. Your collective strength and resilience are #blackgirl magic on steroids. Your examples of triumph in the face of insurmountable odds inspire when I get weary. I know that each of you is forever watching over me and your gentle nudges convince me that I can keep moving forward despite any obstacles I may face. Thank you for encouraging me to write and to document my story in my own words.

Thank you to my father, Ron. Although you have passed on, your inquisitive nature and love of reading lives on in me. And to my stepfather, Leon, thank you for standing in the gap and always being a constant source of positivity.

Thank you to my aunts and surrogate moms Lois, Alberta, Belinda, Luvenia, Gwen, Iris, Christine, Gloria, Kathleen, and Robbie. You all have taught me to be fearless, dream big, and live out loud.

Thank you to my brothers, sisters, sister-friends, cousins, and friends for always supporting me in every project and effort upon which I embark. Your love, phone calls, many text messages, and words of encouragement keep me going!

Thank you to my teams at Leaders Press, Special Needs Network, Martin & Martin LLP, TAMCO, and Butterflly. And to the best marketing and public relations team, whoever said "teamwork makes the dream work" must have had all of you in mind.

My sincerest appreciation to you all!

xoxo

About the Author

AREVA MARTIN is an award-winning civil rights attorney, Harvard Law School graduate, talk show host and entrepreneur. A CNN Legal Analyst, Areva is an audience favorite on a list of shows, from *Dr. Phil*, *The Doctors*, *Good Morning America*, and *World News Tonight* to her web-based talk show *The Special Report*. She also co-hosted the daytime syndicated talk show *Face The Truth*. Areva founded the Los Angeles-based law firm, Martin & Martin, LLP, California premier autism nonprofit Special Needs Network, and the health technology company Butterflly Health, Inc. A national best-selling author, Areva has dedicated her fourth book to helping women worldwide recognize, own, and assert their limitless power.

https://arevamartin.com/books/

https://arevamartin.com/books/